# UPRISING

*The Pueblo Indians
and the First American War
for Religious Freedom*

## JAKE PAGE

**RIO NUEVO**
PUBLISHERS

TUCSON, ARIZONA

Rio Nuevo Publishers®
P.O. Box 5250
Tucson, AZ 85703-0250
(520) 623-9558, www.rionuevo.com

Cover Design: Dave Jenney
Text Design: Rudy Ramos
Illustrations: Jake Page
Map: Patti Isaacs
Photographs front and back cover top:
courtesy of Larry Loendorf.

Library of Congress Cataloging-in-Publication Data

Page, Jake.
  Uprising : the Pueblo indians and the first American war for
religious freedom / Jake Page.
     pages cm
  Includes bibliographical references and index.
  ISBN-13: 978-1-933855-92-9
  ISBN-10: 1-933855-92-4
1. Pueblo Revolt, 1680. 2. Pueblo Indians—Wars. 3. Pueblo
Indians—Religion. I. Title.
  E99.P9P26 2013
  978.9'01—dc23                         2013031341

# Contents

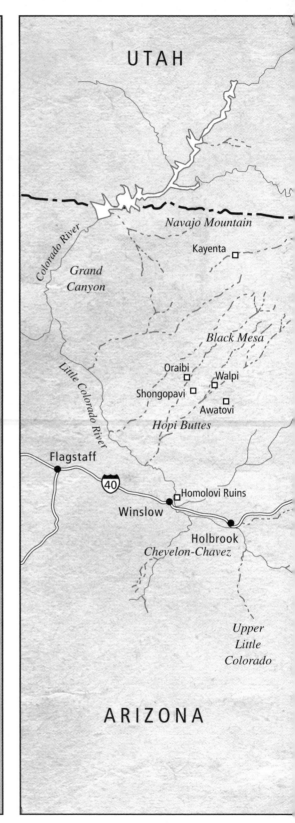

## MAJOR PUEBLOS

*of the*

## REVOLT

*and*

## PUEBLO LANGUAGE GROUPS

✠ ✠ ✠

AREA ENLARGED

- ● Cities
- ■ Modern pueblos
- □ Pueblo ruins
- ▧ Language areas

UTAH

Navajo Mountain

Kayenta □

Colorado River

Grand Canyon

Black Mesa

Oraibi □   Walpi □
Shongopavi □
Awatovi □

Little Colorado River

Hopi Buttes

Flagstaff ●

I-40

Homolovi Ruins □
Winslow ●
Holbrook ●
Chevelon-Chavez

Upper Little Colorado

ARIZONA

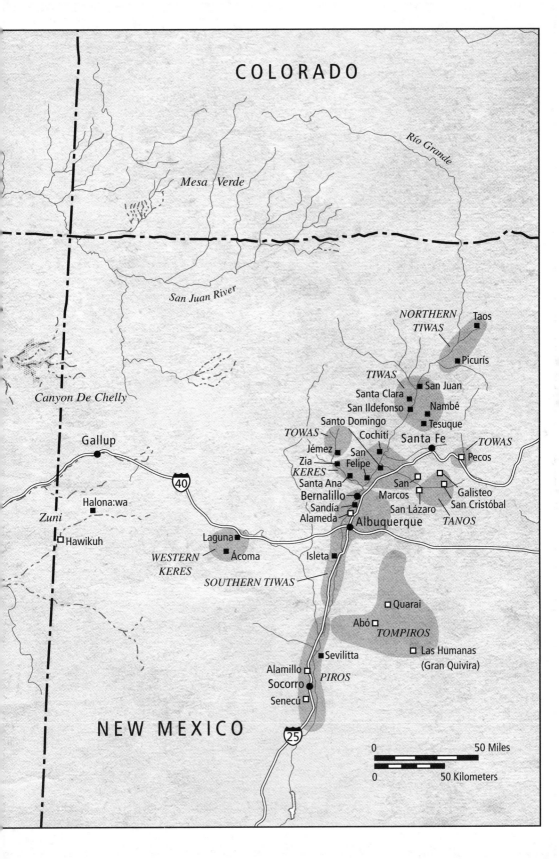

COLORADO

*Río Grande*

*Mesa Verde*

*San Juan River*

*Canyon De Chelly*

Gallup

■ Halona:wa

*Zuni*

□ Hawikuh

I-40

NEW MEXICO

Laguna
□
*WESTERN
KERES*
■ Ácoma

*SOUTHERN TIWAS*

*NORTHERN
TIWAS* ■ Taos

■ Picurís

*TIWAS*

Santa Clara ■ ■ San Juan

San Ildefonso ■ Nambé ■

Santo Domingo ■ Tesuque ■

*TOWAS* ■ Cochití ■

Jémez ■ Santa Fe ● *TOWAS*

Zia ■ San □ Pecos

*KERES* Felipe ■

Santa Ana ■ San □ □

Bernalillo ● Marcos □ Galisteo

Sandía □ San Cristóbal

Alameda □ San Lázaro

Albuquerque ● *TANOS*

Isleta ■

□ Quarai

Abó □ *TOMPIROS*

□ Las Humanas
(Gran Quivira)

■ Sevilitta

Alamillo □ *PIROS*

Socorro ●

Senecú □

I-25

0 ⊢ 50 Miles

0 ⊢ 50 Kilometers

# Introduction

*Conquered by you, the New World has conquered you in turn.*
—JUSTUS LIPSIUS, sixteenth century Stoicist philosopher

SANTA FE, AUGUST 10, 1680—Well before dawn broke the darkness, the Franciscan friar Juan Bautista Pío set out from Santa Fe, the provincial capital of New Mexico, to say mass for the Indian residents of the pueblo of Tesuque, some three leagues (ten miles) to the north. To his simple blue robe and the cross around his neck, he had added a leather shield.

It may have been quite chilly. Nights in this near-desert region are too dry to hold the warmth of the previous day. Father Pío would arrive in Tesuque before the sun became oppressive to him and Pedro Hidalgo, the soldier who accompanied him on horseback. Hidalgo was assigned to protect the Franciscan. Rumors of rebellion were in the air, apprehensions of coming violence whispering like the wind across the mesas and through the valleys and mountains of this most remote and—many thought—godforsaken colony in all of New Spain.

Pedro Hidalgo was armed with the normal complement of weapons for an enlisted man in the Spanish military, a sword and dagger and most notably an harquebus, a cumbersome flintlock musket that the Spanish had invented, the first gun to be fired from the shoulder. Hidalgo was one of only a hundred soldiers in New Mexico called on to maintain peace between a couple of thousand Spanish ranchers, farmers, and holy brothers, and the sixteen thousand Native Americans who lived in the vast, unforgiving, and isolated province.

The two Spaniards might have looked something like Don Quixote and Sancho Panza off to tilt at windmills (in the book then popular in the mother country) except that Fray Pío was on foot, a standard penance among this most

1

*Harquebus*

penitential of brotherly orders. They proceeded through the piñon pines and dark green desert junipers sprinkled here and there on the dusty rolling land like the spots of a jaguar. The sun rose behind the mountains that lay to their east—mountains that would later be called the Sangre de Cristos, meaning the blood of Christ. The new sun cast a pastel glow over the sky, which ripened to a bright yellow and as quickly faded into deep blue–a rapid transition from dark to light, as if the sun were impatient to get on with the new day.

The Franciscan and his guard knew that one of the Hispanic residents of the Tesuque pueblo, a man named Cristóbal Herrera, had been killed in the pueblo the night before. Perhaps it was a sign of worse things to come, as with the rumors, or perhaps it was just a squabble over something (a woman, maybe) that had grown out of control. Such things happened, after all. Nothing ever seemed certain in this country—this world of *perhaps*—except the sun. In any event, Fray Pío, ever devoted to his calling, believed he knew how to calm the people of Tesuque, and, if they were in a seditious mood, persuade them to put aside such thoughts and join in the fellowship of the Holy Mass.

As they neared the pueblo, they saw its mud brick homes, some two stories high, some three stories, rising among the cottonwood trees along the dry wash that, briefly in spring and early summer, ran wet. Drawing closer, they were greeted by an eerie silence. No children squealed and played in the plaza at the town's center. No smoke rose from the buildings, taking off the chill of night. Inside the rectangular plaza, they found the pueblo deserted—an extremely ominous finding.

They pressed on, looking for the inhabitants. A mile outside the pueblo, the two Spaniards descended into a shallow sandy ravine, passing between two low, rounded hills, when they saw some of the villagers, their faces painted red. Hidalgo recognized two of them, a man the Spanish called El Obi and the other, Nicolás, a capable translator.

In Spanish, the Friar Pío cried out: "What is this, children? Are you mad? Do not disturb yourselves. I will die a thousand deaths for you."[1]

Impetuously, he plunged further into the ravine and around a corner, disappearing from the sight of his protector, Pedro Hidalgo. After a few moments, Hidalgo saw El Obi round the bend, carrying the friar's shield, followed by Nicolas, who was spattered with blood. Others swarmed out of the ravine after him. Certain the Franciscan had been martyred, Hidalgo spurred his horse into motion. On foot, the angry Natives closed the distance, tugging at Hidalgo's weapons, but he and the horse lunged out of their grasp and galloped back to Santa Fe. Pedro Hidalgo alerted the provincial governor, Antonio de Otermín, at seven in the morning that the rumored uprising had evidently begun.

This was the first recorded event in the only war that American Indians ever won against the Europeans.

## *European Beginnings*

That day in August, the Pueblo people of the northern Rio Grande and points west exploded in fury, rising up to drive the Spanish military, colonists, and Franciscan missionaries all the way back into New Spain (today's Mexico). Except, that is, for the four hundred or so colonists and Franciscans whom they slaughtered.

Before this uprising, elsewhere in North America, small groups of Europeans had been driven away by American Indians, but in circumstances about which we know very little. Shortly after AD 1000, for example, Leif Eriksson's brief attempt to establish a settlement on Newfoundland was scuttled without noticeable impact outside of a few stray artifacts and a small ruin at Danse aux Meadows. The native people there were the Beothuk tribe–called *skraelings* by the Norse, and now long since extinct as a group. It seems that they played some role in discouraging this handful of the most feared adventurers of medieval Europe.

Half a millennium later, in 1513, Ponce de León left Cuba with a small crew and reached the Florida peninsula ninety miles north. A story about a fountain of youth may have been somewhere in his mind, but his chief interest was the capture of slaves. Instead, he ran into some warriors who forced him to make a hasty retreat to Cuba. These were more than likely Calusa people of southwestern Florida, who had made of their watery world one of the most sophisticated societies ever to subsist entirely on seafood, and who were the dominant force among the local tribes. It may well have been the Calusas who put an abrupt and violent end to León's life when he made the mistake of returning a few years later. Like the Beothuks, the Calusas are long extinct, their mounded villages and elaborate canals through the Everglades depopulated by European diseases and, later, onslaughts of Spanish colonizers.

But these outbreaks were mere skirmishes, nothing that could remotely be called a war, or even a rebellion. Not until 1680 did American Indians drive established European colonists out of their territory—and after that it never happened again.

Even so, the Pueblo Revolt remains little known outside of the American Southwest. This is part of an odd east-coast bias in the minds of many, if not most, Americans, who see the Europeans landing on the east coast in Jamestown, Virginia, and Plymouth, Massachusetts, multiplying there in the thirteen colonies and then heading west over the Appalachians, into Kentucky (Daniel Boone), clearing the Great Plains of Sioux and Cheyenne, and winding up in California with Manifest Destiny complete and the Native tribes pretty much out of luck everywhere. It didn't actually happen that way though.

By 1608, when John Smith and others established the Jamestown colony, Spanish colonists had been living in New Mexico for a decade and two years later would establish the town of Santa Fe as their provincial capital, making it the oldest continuous European settlement in the United States.

What is sometimes also billed as the Pueblo-Spanish War was not a straightforward problem between a native group and a European group, as when the English Puritans set out to rid the world of the Pequot tribe and almost succeeded, or when several New England tribes rose up and attempted to run the Puritans into the sea, and almost succeeded in what is called King Philip's War in the 1690s. By 1680, only eighty-two years after the first Spanish colonists arrived there, what we now call the American Southwest was the most diverse jumble of language groups, cultures, and social, religious, and political systems on the continent.

There were Castilians, Basques, and other Spanish, *mestizos* (Spanish and Mexican Indian mixes), *Genízarros* (some who were Plains mixes), mulattos (blacks and Mexican Indians), Spanish and Pueblo mixes, and so on, all with different social standing. In all, the Pueblo people spoke some nine languages, and the Apaches in the surrounding area yet another. And in this mix—what can properly be thought of as the first American melting pot—intrigue, greed, miscommunication, plots within plots, and interracial, intertribal, even intervillage suspicions and aspirations were all a constant part of the fabric of life.

This was no simple war. Even today some extremist Hispanics in New

Mexico refuse to call it a war or a revolt but instead refer to it as the Saint Lawrence Day Massacre, which, from their point of view, it was.

## *About the Sources*

A note on sources is in order here.

To begin with, the Pueblo people left no written records of any of this for the obvious reason that theirs were not written languages. The Franciscans may well have taught some of their Indian charges as children to write and read Spanish, but if they wrote anything like accounts of daily life, which is unlikely, those were lost long ago. Most western historians or archaeologists don't think much of oral histories of such long-ago events, and most Pueblo people keep such accounts pretty much to themselves, as they do with most aspects of their cultures. What Indian people these days have so far written about their rebellion is mostly congratulatory, rather than expository.

So most of what we know about the Pueblo Rebellion comes from Spanish accounts, which are at worst self-serving and misleading, and at best one-sided for obvious and not so obvious reasons. Not so obvious is that the Spanish and the Franciscans were so preoccupied with the diabolical omnipresence of Satan that, once they accepted that Native Americans were human (though in need of a lot of work), they blamed all their differences from Spanish humans on the Devil and never thought to look into Indian culture very deeply. Indeed, their job was to stamp out such "devilish cultural practices," not to study them. And the Indian rituals seemed so diabolical that it was best not even to watch them: they believed they were in a sense spiritually toxic. Conversely, the Pueblo people, like any occupied people, probably told the Spanish and the friars whatever they thought they wanted to hear, but not anything important.

Another problem in mutual understanding was the matter of language. The Pueblos, especially children, were required by the Franciscans to learn Spanish. But even if the Indians had wanted to explain certain concepts, especially ceremonial ones, to the Spanish, they probably would not have found the needed words in the Spanish language. The Spanish in the New World took a very dim view of Indian languages. For example, a professor at the University of Mexico in 1585 wrote that they "appear to have been introduced not by men but by nature, as the illiterate noise of birds or brute animals, which cannot be written down with any kind of character, and can scarcely be pronounced for being so guttural that they stick in the throat." Very few Franciscans in New Mexico tried to overcome these difficulties.

What historians have been left with are chiefly Spanish administrative records and the writings of the friars. In the 1500s, the Spanish under King Philip II had created out of whole cloth the world's first major bureaucracy in order to manage the affairs of an empire that stretched around the world from Europe to the New World to the Philippines—an empire larger than even that of Rome in its heyday. These bureaucrats were unbelievably wordy and assiduous to a fault in record-keeping.

Sadly, all the government archives in Santa Fe were burned during the rebellion. So the Spanish side of things comes from copies of documents that found their way to archives in Durango, Mexico City, and Madrid. These have been laboriously searched out and pieced together by historians over the past two centuries, and have been augmented by the records of the friars (and in particular the Inquisition) in New Mexico that were sent back to the Franciscan headquarters in Mexico City. It is on the shoulders of these scholars, and what is probably an incomplete collection of documents, that all subsequent historians have stood—and read between the lines.

Lately, scholars in other fields have been making contributions to the overall story. Archaeologists have studied settlement patterns and other trends that can speak from silent ruins and artifacts in the ground about changing Indian approaches to the occupation of their lands and lives. An old pot can tell what one Indian woman may have thought about the Spanish rule. Ethnohistorians and anthropologists have made the best of suggesting the nature of Indian cultures now and perhaps then—though few such scholars feel comfortable speculating back in time based on evidence of today.

## Pueblo Lifeways and Beliefs

On the other hand, we can be pretty sure about certain conditions back then in spite of the fact that they have almost nothing in common with our lives today. We put meat on the table, for example, in a neat and bloodless way: few of us kill the animal, get blood on ourselves as we butcher it, and devour its many parts. In those days, quite normal people killed living things all the time to survive. The only vegetarians were deer and other grazers. Blood was a daily item.

There were no deodorants in those days. People bathed infrequently. They stank, and you did not *put up* with it any more than fish put up with water. It was simply part of the scene. Many pregnancies were not full term. Infants died frequently, and to this day many Indian cultures do not give a baby a name until a few weeks after its birth, when it looks like the child has a good chance of surviving. A prematurely born infant would almost certainly die unnamed and, hopefully, find a new body for its spirit to inhabit. Balancing the spirit world was a major concern.

## *Forces of Good and Evil*

Everyone was situated amid a constant flux of palpable, active forces of good and evil—an eternal war. Today, many of us permit evil to be defined as entropy and disorder, or genetic glitches, or bad parenting. In those days, evil was Evil. The Spanish, as noted, believed that Satan lurked everywhere, vying for possession of your soul against the power of the Son of God, who was ever-present in the ubiquitous symbolism of the Cross. For the Indian people, the spirits of nature and other phenomena went both ways: they could help or harm. For virtually everyone present in New Mexico in those days, Good and Evil represented the true dual nature of the world. And worse, certain people sometimes called shamans could harness the essential workings of evil (as well as those of good). Witchcraft—particularly the doing of evil to one another—was for both the Spanish and the Indians another way to understand the very real and otherwise unexplainable visitations of disease, terror, terrible luck (but mainly disease) that were the handmaidens of daily life. Witchcraft, to digress on an important topic, is altogether a common presence in the minds and affairs of the Indians of the Southwest to this day. It is a very serious and often lethal business. Some FBI agents in Gallup, New Mexico, once told me they would not investigate witchcraft murders on the Navajo reservation (which today surrounds the Hopi lands) because there was never any forensic, medical, or other court-acceptable evidence to explain what had happened (in other words, the cause of death) and who was guilty.

## *The European Experience*

Life in sixteenth-century New Mexico, which included parts of Arizona, was risky and usually short. Octogenarians were rarities and much admired. Death and violence were expected. The Spanish province of New Mexico remained for all intents and purposes in the late Middle Ages, not growing into the Reformation or the Renaissance that had begun to bloom in Italy and elsewhere in Europe. It was a time when people in Europe had only recently begun to think in terms of "nations," when Indians saw themselves as groups more local and intimate than "tribes." Not every European in the New World shared the belief stated by the Spanish king and the Pope that Indians were, in fact, humans and not just human-like beings without souls.

Life was also much slower then. Information from the political and administrative center of New Spain typically traveled at the speed of an ox-drawn cart or, at best, a horse. The Pueblo Indians were great long-distance runners, legendarily covering as much as sixty miles in a day.

In New Mexico, no one conceived of the notion of progress as we think of it today. Beyond the addition of some Spanish tools and foods to New Mexico, technological change was imperceptible—for Indian and colonist alike. This was a small-town world where kindnesses or slights were remembered for centuries. How small-town? The provincial capital of Santa Fe was home to about 1,500 people, of whom half or more were low-class who lived across the river in the first barrio to exist in what would one day be the United States. The largest community of local Indians was the pueblo of Pecos with some two thousand people, about the size of a high school of today.

Most people, including most of the Spanish colonists, were illiterate. The main form of communication was word-of-mouth—in other words, gossip and rumor.

It was in this world, Spain's most remote, least-loved and least promising province, that what can legitimately be called the first American revolution took place. The war and its aftermath were what people sometimes call a watershed event. This metaphor seems a bit out of place, however, given the paucity of moisture in the American Southwest. I prefer to think of the revolt as the waist of an hourglass through which regional Indian and Spanish history had to pass before it could continue and expand into yet wider realms.

It was, to be sure, a local event, but so was the battle that brought an end to the life of General Custer at the Little Bighorn about a century later, and it was surely as well planned if not more so, as any other Native American battle or uprising.

## New Approaches

Why write this book on the Pueblo Rebellion when many already exist? Most of them are for scholars, for one thing, powerfully researched and well written, if densely. The books most accessible to the public do not go very far in explaining what happened after the Pueblo Rebellion—for one thing, a second rebellion. And most of them have little to say about the role of the Hopis in any of this, those most western and otherwise remote of the participants. Over the years, my wife and I have spent a great deal of time among the Hopis, and they have been more forthcoming than most of the Indian participants in the rebellion about themselves, their ways of thinking about the world, their ceremonial practices, and their roles in the rebellion and its aftermath. They are the closest we can come, given what the Pueblo Indians of today are willing to talk about, to get any fine detail on what might have been in the minds of the rebels for all those years.

Having been let in on some matters that most people don't learn about, I feel fairly confident about elaborating on some of the historical reports and other findings about the Pueblos* with insights from Susanne's and my experiences at Hopi, and also in New Mexico, where we lived for sixteen years.

Finally, it seems to me that anyone with an appreciation of the American Indians and their contributions to American life, art, and spirituality should have a working knowledge of one of the most important events in all of American Indian history—if only as an exercise in common courtesy.

---

\*   I have tried to consistently refer to the towns as pueblos and the people living in them as Pueblos. The alternative is to call them Puebloans, which seems a bit dry and academic sounding. The Hopis refuse the term pueblo (and Pueblo) because it's a Spanish word and the Hopis are extreme apostates. They live in what they call "villages" when speaking in English.

# PART ONE

# BEGINNINGS

# CHAPTER 1

# The Seven Cities of Gold

THE FIRST NON-INDIAN to confront the ancestors of the Pueblo rebels was not who they all came to call "the white man." He was instead a black man known by a host of variations on the name Estéban. Evidently a black Arab from Morocco, he was a slave—and a slave with an attitude. In 1528, he was among the few survivors of a Spanish expedition from Cuba that foundered in Florida and made its way with primitive watercraft to Galveston, Texas.

From there, with three Spaniards, Estéban made his way on foot around the Gulf of Mexico, an epic trek that took eight years during which Estéban and his companions were mostly captives of successive tribes along what is now the Texas coast. Finally, in 1536, they arrived in the colonial capital of New Spain, then simply called Mexico. It had previously been the seat of the Aztec empire, done in by Cortés and smallpox.

Along the way, Estéban became something of a self-styled shaman and healer, mimicking both the native shamans and the healing ceremonies of the Catholic Church. Once in New Spain, he and his companions told stories of great cities and great wealth of the native tribes they had encountered, which fed the desire for that wondrous metal, gold, and of equal desirability, silver—a desire that burned so feverishly in the Spanish colonial soul. This was only three decades after the Spanish, under Hernando Cortés, had arrived in today's Mexico.

In early 1539, Estéban accompanied a small expedition led by a Franciscan, Fray Marcos de Niza, north into the desert highlands to find and inspect these fabled cities and to further the other Spanish passion, the conversion of heathens to the Way of the Cross. Pushing ahead of the rest, Estéban and a few Mexican Indian auxiliaries proceeded through the Sonoran desert, a place of giant cacti, on through mountains green with ponderosa pine forests, and into the arid lands of the Zunis, an area of mesas and plains south of present-day Gallup, New Mexico. All along the way, Estéban dispatched tantalizing messages back to Fray Marcos.

In this earliest boosterism of the American West, a Zuni town called Hawikuh would soon become Cibola, and Cibola would soon blossom into a kingdom of seven cities, the fabled seven cities of gold that had long lain just out of sight in the Spanish psyche and myth.

But when Estéban reached Hawikuh, the main Zuni settlement, he found a single large, multi-family dwelling of several stories, not unlike a house made from individual blocks, spread out in a rectangle on the ground with blocks piled on top for five stories altogether. Each room was accessible only by a ladder through its roof. Built from adobe bricks, which are chiefly concocted out of mud and water, this huge apartment building of landscape-mirroring brown was surely impressive, but it is easy to imagine how disappointing it must have been to the conquistadors, who probably hoped for something like the cities of the Aztecs, which were comparable in architectural magnificence and wealth to such European cities as Venice. In the land surrounding the great apartment building of the Zunis there were wonderfully green fields where corn, beans, and squash grew, watered by a small river that coursed through Zuniland and supported four other such "towns."

Approaching what was essentially a Zuni apartment building, Estéban crossed (inadvertently, one imagines) a line of cornmeal sprinkled across the town's entrance, placed there most likely to welcome back some Zuni priests who were off on a pilgrimage to outlying shrines. Such pilgrimages are not uncommon today. When crossing the line of cornmeal, either coming or going, one needs to pause and pray. Not to do so is a serious affront. No doubt something like that happened at Zuni

*Hopi shield design*

that day long ago. Clearly, Estéban did not understand the gravity of the mistake he made in barging across the sacred line, but he then exacerbated an unfortunate introduction by brazenly demanding tribute of turquoise, gold, and women.

It is not clear whether the Zunis executed this rude and presumptuous alien on the spot or imprisoned him and executed him three days later. Being a deliberative sort, the Zunis probably thought about it a while before taking any final action. But whatever happened exactly, Estéban was executed, and early contact—by more of a con man than a conquistador—ended poorly, an omen of things to come.

Learning of Estéban's murder, Fray Marcos beat a hasty retreat to New Spain, spreading word of a city to the north larger than the city of Mexico. The Spanish bureaucracy, though already of considerable size and inertial weight, acted quickly once it heard in 1539 of these northern riches. The Viceroy, the king's representative in New Spain, appointed Francisco Vásquez de Coronado, a young provincial governor, to assemble and lead a huge expedition north to conquer these promising territories and find the fabled gold. Coronado assembled a vast caravan of three hundred splendidly mounted officers and foot soldiers, all of them youthful and seeking fortunes, plus Fray Marcos and a handful of other friars, along with fifteen hundred head of horses, sheep, cattle, and swine. The expedition started out in late 1539 with typical Spanish pageantry and fanfare, banners aloft, and it had about a thousand miles to go.

Such expeditions were typically financed and outfitted by private money, though usually also enjoying authorization from the Spanish crown. Coronado, like earlier conquistadors, was essentially a venture explorer whose backers expected a return on their investment. Even though his main funding came from his wealthy wife's holdings, the profit motive was just as great. At the same time, he (like all other Spanish adventurers in the New World) was under royal orders to explore and take possession of these northern lands but to do no harm to the native populations. The Spanish crown also desired that some members of these exploratory missions remain as colonists and that the native population be "reduced" (meaning re-led, or persuaded, to live in villages rather than roaming far and wide, thus easier to be converted to Christianity). Such regulations had been in effect for several decades, but since New Spain was a long way from the royal court, the call for treating the Indians with kindness rather than hostility was often observed more in the breach.

Coronado's caravan arrived at Hawikuh, the main Zuni residence, on July 7, 1540, no doubt having been observed by Apaches hidden in the rugged mountains and mesas and probably having also been spotted by Zunis days before they arrived. July is hot and dry in the Southwest, and the caravan's dust plume would have been visible from far off. The Zunis greeted the Spaniards with bows and arrows and demanded that they go away. A ferocious fight ensued, with harquebus fire winning the day and the Zunis ending up arrow-less, throwing rocks at the invaders. Finally they fled, joining their women and children who had already been sent into the mountains.

Finding nothing like a city, much less one of gold, Coronado sent Fray Marcos home, calling him a liar for all his patent falsehoods. But Coronado stayed at Hawikuh for five months nonetheless, surviving comfortably on the pueblo's stores of corn, beans, and cucurbits (squash and gourds), along with its turkeys (the only domesticated animals in North America except for dogs). The Zunis returned during this occupation and an uneasy truce existed. A delegation of Indians arrived one day from the far-off Pecos pueblo on the other side of a great river. Traditional trading people, they wanted a glimpse of the newcomers and what they might have to trade.

Coronado heard about many villages on that great river to the east, and the Zunis had already mentioned the existence of what might be the Seven Cities to the north—the villages of the Hopis, the sometimes friends, sometimes rivals of the Zuni people. A lieutenant with a small complement of soldiers was sent to explore, subdued some hostile Hopis, and went on to become the first Europeans to see the Grand Canyon. Coronado also sent a detail to the great river (the Rio Grande), which flowed past numerous pueblos and neatly farmed fields. The Spanish detail traveled as far north as Taos, receiving warm welcomes along the way. They also went east to return the visit of Pecos people, finding a large pueblo where two thousand people lived on the edge of the buffalo plains.

Coronado then moved his headquarters to a place well to the east of Zuni and just north of present-day Albuquerque, the realm of several small pueblos inhabited by people speaking the Tiwa language, evidently the reason why Coronado called the place Tiguez. Here, the Indians and now the Spaniards could look to the east where the Sandia mountains rose up, crouching over the valley like a huge guard dog. These pueblos were nothing like the size of Pecos. Instead they were small, sometimes two-story affairs in which a hundred or so people lived.

The initial welcome with which the Tiguez people greeted Coronado wore out quite soon. Winter had arrived and it was the kind of bone-chilling cold that often occurs in the desert. The great number of Spaniards, Mexican Indian auxiliaries, and hungry livestock soon strained the Tiguez stores. Some of the intruders even went so far as to steal clothes off Tiguez backs. At one Tiguez pueblo called Arenal, the Indians, outraged by an unpunished rape of one of their women, stampeded a Spanish herd of horses, killing some of them. In order to make a forceful and frightening example, Coronado had Arenal laid waste after a two-day siege, its escaping people rounded up and killed. But the Pueblos fought on into the spring, by which time the Christians had burned hundreds of warriors at the stake and some ten or more pueblos had been abandoned. Just exactly where all these Tiguez pueblos were located remains unknown, but it is thought that some were on the west of the Rio Grande, some possibly on the east. One such pueblo, however, called Kuaua, a Tiwa word for evergreen, has been excavated and to some extent restored, including a ceremonial room called a kiva with several murals from this period. The ruins are now, with a wondrous irony, called the Coronado State Monument.

While visiting Pecos, the Spaniards heard of a place of great riches well to the east out on the Great Plains. Their interlocutor was a Plains Indian resident at Pecos whom they called "the Turk" because he looked like one. He claimed to be from Quivira, a place of much gold and silver out on the plains to the east. So Coronado took most of his expedition onto the plains to investigate the Turk's claims. Led by the Turk, they evidently traveled some five hundred miles, as far as a Wichita Indian village on the Arkansas River in central Kansas. There, they learned that the Turk had been asked by the Pecos Pueblos to lead the aliens on a long march to a place where they would be lost in the vastness of the ocean of grass and they would be doomed. They promptly garroted the Turk, and Coronado headed back to the Río del Norte. Suffering a severe head trauma from being kicked by one of his horses, he gave up on the expedition altogether. He had to be carried back to New Spain in 1542, lying in a litter slung between two mules, with nothing to show but some more or less vague geographical information.

Tried in Mexico City for bad management, Coronado was exonerated by the court, perhaps because he was a broken man, his personality much altered by the blow to his head. He died in relative disgrace twelve years after his return to face the court. The bloom was off the rose as far as New Mexico was concerned. There was good country up north, to be sure, but it was good only for ranching and farming. And the Spanish Empire had no shortage of that sort of wealth.

## Height of the Spanish Empire

To put Coronado's expedition in global context, in his time explorers from New Spain had extended their range well up the California coast, and others from Caribbean outposts like Cuba had sailed most of the coast of the Gulf of Mexico and the Florida peninsula, extending as far north as Virginia on the Atlantic coast. A Spanish mission was established north of the site of Jamestown in 1570 (thirty-seven years ahead of John Smith), but it lasted only a year.

Indeed, the reach of the Spanish Empire was at its greatest in this very period, stretching from the Iberian Peninsula around the world to the Philippines, eastward across the Pacific to Mexico and Peru, and encompassing the entire Caribbean including the Florida Peninsula, as well as the Netherlands, in Europe. The Spanish king, Philip II, was the master of the largest and most efficient bureaucracy ever known to that time, necessary to administer the first global empire. The empire was still in its heyday, but that would not last very far into the next century. In 1588, the Spanish king sent the greatest fleet of warships ever assembled up to that point in history to put an end to the competition of the English. The unexpected result was the humiliating defeat of the Spanish Armada, a major psychological blow as well as military, and a sign that in the rivalries of the European nations, Spain was among equals.

# CHAPTER 2

# Pageantry at the Northward Passage

ON APRIL 30, 1598, Ascension Day, four hundred Spanish men, a few of them soldiers and Franciscan friars, and a hundred and thirty Spanish women stood in a cottonwood-lined oasis on the south side of the Río Bravo del Norte not far below what is today the city of El Paso, Texas. There, across the muddy river, Don Juan de Oñate, the leader of this expedition, formally took possession of the lands to the north, already called Nuevo México. He claimed those lands in the name of the royal king of Castile and the holy Pontiff and Jesus Christ. To the south lay the desert they had crossed, and to the north more desert to cross before arriving in the new Promised Land.

A pole with a colorful standard and topped with a silver cross arose over Oñate's head as he took possession of the land. On the front of this flag presided the Virgin of Remedies, patron saint of the Spanish in the city then called Mexico. On the other side were the gold castles of Castile on a red background and the red lions of León on white. As the Franciscan Fray Angelico Chavez would write almost four hundred years later, "All emblems together portray the *anima hispanica,* the Spanish soul, coming upon new pasture."

Don Juan de Oñate had been a logical choice to fund and lead this grand expedition. He was nearly fifty years old, the experienced scion of a fabulously wealthy silver mine owner in Zacatecas, now making up for lower yields from Peru. His wife was the granddaughter of Hernán Cortés, and the great-granddaughter of the wife of the Aztec ruler Montezuma—as close as the New World would ever come to producing a true aristocrat. Oñate was no greedy adventurer but a man of stature, indeed something of a noble of New Spain in his own right.

While Oñate's family was originally Basque, as were a few other members of the expedition, most of the leading participants were originally Castilian. Castile is in the highlands of Spain, a relatively desolate landscape that is terrifically hot in the summer, and then terrifically cold in the winter. The philosopher Miguel de Unamuno wrote of the Castilian landscape as "uniform in its contrasts of light and shade, in its unblended colors bereft of intermediary tints . . . [of its] immense plateau and the density of blue which spreads over it and gives it light."[2] He went on to say that this "infinite countryside is, if we might put it so, a landscape which is monotheistic instead of pantheistic."

*Detail of Oñate family crest*

As Fray Chavez pointed out, this could be a description of Palestine, the ancient region that gave rise to Abraham and Jesus, and it could also be a description of New Mexico's landscape—except for one thing. New Mexico was already inhabited, as the Spanish well knew, by people of a distinctly pantheistic bent. In any event, the members of Oñate's expedition, who had ridden or walked for months across barren lands to reach this place, identified themselves with the biblical lands as well as with Castile, and a deep evangelical purpose had borne them across the wilderness they had just left behind.

Taking possession of the lands that lay ahead, records show, Oñate prayed: "Open the door of heaven to these heathens, establish the church and altars where the body and the blood of the son of God may be offered, open to us the way to security and peace for their preservation and ours, and give to our king, and to me in his royal name, peaceful possession of these kingdoms and provinces for His blessed glory. Amen."[3]

After Oñate's words died away, after the High Mass and the sermon, and after the trumpets had fallen silent, some of the soldiers put on a drama for everyone to enjoy. The play spoke most eloquently to the sacred evangelical goal—to save the souls of the heathens whom Coronado had seen, as had a few others who had made their way—albeit briefly—into the realm of the pueblos.

In 1573, Philip II, appalled at what he had heard about some individuals brutalizing the Indians, issued orders that prohibited unauthorized expeditions into new lands, and forbade the use of the word "conquest" for what were pacifications. The royal orders made missionaries the leaders of such expeditions. In 1581, a Franciscan, Fray Agustín Rodríguez, led two other friars and seven soldiers to the Pueblo world, believing themselves to be the first Spaniards to do so. Fray Agustín was looking for new Indians to convert, a task that the Spanish king heartily supported. In New Mexico, the Rodriguez group named the area San Felipe del Nuevo México. When the expedition turned back, two friars elected to stay and get to work converting the Pueblo people.

The following year, a man who was more of an adventurer than an explorer, Antonio de Espejo, got permission to head north in order, he said, to rescue the two friars. But when he arrived, he found that they had been killed, going off to their maker under the most holy of circumstances, as martyrs. Espejo roamed into the plains and across much of Arizona. Though he found no gold or silver, and though he, like Coronado, had felt the need to capture and kill a significant number of Indians, he returned to New Spain with tales of a wonderful country to be colonized, with mineral resources and clean and hard-working Indians to help. There were other visits, mostly brief and largely unimportant. When Philip II heard of all this, he requested that the Viceroy of New Spain appoint someone to lead a major expedition with the goal of establishing a new colony and converting the Indians there to Christianity.

A certain urgency hung over this expedition, felt by the Crown in Madrid as well as by the Viceroy of New Spain. The great silver mines of Mexico and Peru were becoming less productive, meaning less silver was being transshipped to Madrid via the port city of Seville. To make mercantile matters worse, the inhabitants of New Spain now were producing most of the material goods they needed themselves, no longer dependent on the markets in Seville. But sales aside, it was, in great part, the New World's silver that was the lifeblood of the Spanish imperial efforts to rule all of Europe, not to mention its far-flung colonies, an effort that was both secular and religious.

Spain saw itself as the right arm of the Vatican and had taken on the task of forestalling, indeed, pushing back the spread of dreaded Protestantism from England and the Netherlands. But as Oñate set out for the north in 1598, Spain had already suffered some reversals, the loss of the armada for one, but far worse, it would turn out, was that Philip II, the steady hand that for decades had presided over the Spanish expansion, died in 1598. People were largely aware that his son Philip III was no match for his father's enlightened command of political affairs. Though art would flourish under Philip III with famous painters of the royal court, such as Velasquez, the new king delegated functioning of the empire to cronies.

In 1598, bankruptcy forced the Spanish Crown to seek peace with France, and in the ensuing decade Spain would be forced to seek peace with both England and later the Netherlands. Meanwhile, in 1599–1600, famine and plague struck Castile and Andalusia, killing off half a million people from a population of six million. (By way of contrast, in 1598, the population of all of New Spain was about a quarter of a million.)

It took a good deal of time, but finally Juan de Oñate was selected to raise the funds needed and to lead the expedition called for by Philip II. Thus, the *entrada* of colonization arrived in late spring of the unpromising year 1598 on the threshold of this new world in the New World. And the play the soldiers put on included the dramatic story of Fray Rodríguez and the other two friars, showing them achieving martyrdom. Shortly afterward, the assembled colonists-to-be crossed over in a place a few miles upstream where the river, swollen from runoff from mountains that lay far beyond the northern horizon, could be forded, a place they called El Paso del Norte.

In Madrid, hopes ran high that Oñate's entrada would lead to the early discovery of the silver and gold promise of the new lands to the north, but even had such finds occurred, it appeared (as historian J. H. Elliott has pointed out) that like Spain's most famous fictional hero, Don Quixote (soon to arrive on the scene), in 1605 the Spanish empire had lost its bearings in a changing world.

## The Franciscan Order

It is time to pause in these complex imperial and colonial affairs and ask just who were the Franciscans, these men in the blue robes cinched with a simple strand of rope, who carried a staff and walked the world in sandals, whose only "decoration" was a cross swinging from a chain or string around the neck? Why did the Spanish throne entrust to them the souls and lives of so many (indeed, countless) native people in this newly discovered hemisphere? Why had the Spanish throne given the responsibility for planting a Spanish brand of civilization among these savages to these few men sometimes called the Little Brothers, whose allegiance became over time first and last to Jesus Christ and the Church? These men practiced what amounted to an extra-national loyalty—loyalty less to the King of Spain than to the Pope.

To begin with, the Franciscans were the Catholic order founded by the Middle Age's most Christlike saint, Francis Bernadone, who lived in the Italian city of Assisi. He was born in 1182, the son of a successful merchant and his noble wife, and he became a spoiled, degenerate romantic and carouser who dreamed of becoming a knight like Lancelot. He tried the crafts of knighthood, got wounded and humiliated in the process, and had an overpowering religious conversion, vowing to give up all the trappings of modern life and become as much like Christ as he could. He took up begging for a living and preached the truth of Christ, extolling and practicing love for all creatures. So saintly was he that the stigmata appeared on his hands and feet.

Before long he attracted others of a similar mind (within ten years they numbered about five thousand), and they referred to themselves as The Friars Minor. These were not to be learned monastics like the recently founded order of the Dominicans. They were instead to go forth into the towns and preach. They wore peasant robes, and they often rode, occasionally walked. Nor were they to be ordained priests, but only lay brothers, poor and penitential. But unlike the radical heresies of the time that found the Church too formal and corrupt, the Little Brothers believed fully in the sacraments of the Church and the priests' crucial role, so before long, in 1209, Pope Innocent III authorized them as an Order.

Even before the passing of St. Francis, some of the Franciscans began to change in their attributes and goals, encouraged to do so by the Church hierarchy. They became wandering *priests*, authorized to administer the sacraments. They developed a corporate structure, holding property corporately as an order. They became scholars of philosophy and science: Franciscan scholars became central to the founding universities in Paris and Oxford. They included among their members Oxford's John Dun Scotus, perhaps the greatest medieval logician, and William Occam, also of Oxford, who confirmed Scotus's belief that knowledge of God could arise only from revelation or intuition, not logic. But William is remembered more for giving scientists the Law of Occam's Razor, often quoted to this day, which says that the simplest explanation that fits all the facts is likely to be the right one.

By the end of the thirteenth century, several strains existed within the Franciscan Order, varying chiefly in the intensity of their commitment to total poverty and simplicity. By the time Cortés had conquered the Aztec empire in the 1530s, there were some 55,000 Franciscans, many engaged in preaching and missionary work in far-flung realms including the Middle East, Africa, and the Americas.

Upon the discovery of the New World, major philosophical battles ensued over the status of the Native tribes. Were they rational human beings or something less? And what were the rights of the Spanish in these new territories? It was a Dominican, Bartolomé de Las Casas, who, against formidable opposition in the court of Spain, became the Indians' main champion in the 1500s, strongly opposing their enslavement. He insisted they were rational, perfectly capable of understanding such things as the catechism—that is, they could be and should be converted to Catholicism. He went even further, arguing in lengthy treatises that the Indians should be converted only peacefully, not by force, and also that lands taken illegally from them, meaning by force, should be returned to them.

Yet some took a more pessimistic view of the capabilities of the Indians. The Bishop of Chiapas was one. He addressed the third Mexican Provincial Council of 1585 in the following terms:

> We must love and help the Indians as much as we can. But their base and imperfect character requires that they should be ruled, governed, and guided to their appointed end by fear more than love . . . These people do not know how to judge the gravity of their sins other than by the rigour of the penalties with which they are punished.[4]

This left room for interpretation by those on the ground far away from the seats of civilization and power.

By the end of the sixteenth century, the job of conversions was just about completed throughout New Spain. The population of souls to be saved had been much reduced by European diseases. Those Franciscans still looking for lives of poverty, loneliness, and danger, with a high likelihood of martyrdom, were drawn by the possibilities of the distant realm, New Mexico. They went there as seriously determined to save pagan souls as the conquistadores were to find the Seven Cities of Gold. And since they believed the Royal Orders for New Discoveries would apply, they would be saving souls of pagans who had not previously been mistreated by Spanish adventurers and soldiers.

The Franciscans who came to the New World were from the more moderate, educated, less zealously poor strain of the order. They were, however, as given to the notion and practice of penitence as any men of God. (The Poor Clares, the sisters associated with the Franciscan order, did not come to the New World till centuries later.)

*Detail of Franciscan insignia. Arms of Jesus and St. Francis. Note stigmata.*

Penitence for the Franciscans took the form of fasting, periods of silence, and, within the privacy of their own cells, scourging themselves. This was not the frantic, self-inflicted, gory wounding practiced by the radical flagellants who popped up all over Europe after the years of the Black Plague, but it was physical punishment—self-inflicted and occasionally drawing blood. Fray Angelico Chávez explained that this was no rite of morbidity but was practiced out of a tragic sense of empathy with the trials of Christ as He passed through the fourteen Stations of the Cross (a Catholic motif greatly emphasized by the Little Brothers). Any hardship or pain inflicted by nature or accident in the course of the holy work was seen as a welcome penitence, suffered in the hope that God would look favorably on the friars' enterprise.

Most of the colonists who came to settle New Mexico saw their journey not only as offering the possibility of an improved life—the promise of becoming a land owner, an *hidalgo*—but also as an offering to God.

Once in New Mexico, the Franciscans believed, they could create their own Kingdom of God, an Eden where the newly converted would live in perfect communal harmony and the friars would live as their founder had— Christlike. They would be the most learned human beings in New Mexico, the most penitential. They would be teachers of the practical arts and crafts to the Indians, bringing to them as well the possibility of life eternal in Paradise. It would be a place where, bravely and joyfully facing the future and whatever hardships it brought, they would be judged by their own avowed standards— St. Francis of Assisi and Jesus Christ.

But they would also be judged, in this miserable province of New Mexico, by the standards of an equally ancient culture, and found wanting.

# CHAPTER 3

# Colonial Birth Pangs

DON JUAN DE OÑATE, having blessed the land before him, crossed the Río Bravo del Norte with his caravan of soldier-colonists, their women, children, and servants, along with ten Franciscans and two lay brothers. They headed north and soon found themselves in one of the eeriest and most inhospitable places in the world. It is a vast area that came to be called *La Jornada del Muerto* (the route of the dead man), a shadeless badland of parched and sun-blasted white sands (consisting of gypsum) and congealed black lava flows and heavily armed plants, with saw-toothed mountains in the distance on either side. Today this is the site of White Sands National Monument, a missile range, a few rumored lost treasures in the mountains, and to the north a place called Trinity where the first atomic bomb was detonated.

After a few days in this terrible place, the Oñate expedition was exhausted and thirsty from extreme, inescapable heat and glare. But the entrance was benevolent overall. They soon came across a friendly young dog, probably an escapee from an Apache hunting party. Tail wagging, it led them to a spring. Later, having marched about a hundred and forty miles northward from their original crossing of the Río del Norte, they came to the river again and saw their first pueblos, hamlets of adobe buildings with tiny emerald fields filled with corn plants—a well-ordered peaceful place, surely a relief after the forbidding badlands they had crossed. There were several of these pueblos strung out along the river, inhabited by people who spoke the Piro tongue. Oñate ceremonially claimed each as a vassal of the Spanish throne and at one of the more northern pueblos they were offered large quantities of corn. They named the pueblo Socorro, referring to the succor they received at the hands of the Piros, and continued north.

Over the next days and weeks, as Oñate's expedition marched north along the wide river, they passed by many trim villages and green fields. At thirty-four of the villages, the residents came out and happily pledged allegiance to the Spanish king, though it is difficult to imagine what they understood by that. At each of these villages, Oñate explained that it was the Spanish king's intention to protect the Indian people from their enemies and to show them how to live for eternity. All they had to do was obey Oñate and the friars. If they did not, they would be severely punished.

By early July, Oñate's caravan reached the place in the north where the great river was joined by another, today called the Chama River, in northern New Mexico. There Oñate established his capital in a pueblo called Ohkay Owingeh (near present-day Española), which the Spanish called San Juan Pueblo. The Spaniards simply moved in, making no effort to build their own dwellings. A year later they would move across the river to another pueblo, forcing its inhabitants to move into San Juan, while they renamed their new "capital" San Gabriel. Clearly, the Pueblos up and down the river had concluded that it made no sense to resist these strangers whose predecessors, well within living memory, had been so destructive.

Oñate immediately set about introducing administrative order into his vast domain—in all what we now know was some eighty-seven thousand square miles of mostly unexplored territory, an area almost twice the size of Pennsylvania. It stretched from the Hopi mesas in present-day northern Arizona, east to the large Pecos pueblo, north to Taos, and south beyond the Piro pueblos to El Paso del Norte. The main feature of this land was the Rio Grande Rift Valley, the second largest in the world after the one in Africa. Like most rift valleys, it gets wider the farther away from the source one goes. North of Taos, the rift is essentially a deep canyon.

At the place where Albuquerque is now, and where Coronado savaged the Tiguez Pueblos, it is about thirty miles wide. Most of the northern pueblos were then and still are to be found in the rift valley or along the subsidiary valleys of smaller rivers feeding into the Rio Grande. The Rio Grande is, by standards set by the Missouri, the Mississippi, or even the Potomac, not much of a river. It is not very deep or wide, its grandeur being from its length—the sixth longest river in the United States, running from the continental divide in southern Colorado to the very southern tip of Texas (that is, when enough water runs through to keep it wet its entire length, a rarity these days).

The Chihuahuan desert covers much of the land from the Tiguez pueblos south to El Paso and farther south. Here there is but one brief rainy season with extremely cold winters and blisteringly hot dry summers. The most prominent plant is the *cholla* cactus, an ugly, multi-branched and powerfully armed cactus that has the reputation of suddenly leaping at the legs of riders. From the Piro pueblos on north, the land is considered not desert but semi-arid, receiving from nine to twelve inches of rain annually, enough along with irrigation to support a much greener world than what lies to the south. It is in these greener places where the pueblos were to be found, many in the subsidiary river basins along streams lined with cottonwood trees and willows.

In these earlier times, grasslands were prolific north of the desert, supporting plenty of wild grazing animals such as deer and pronghorns, and soon to include the Spanish cattle and other livestock. These former grasslands have more recently been totally overgrazed and have turned into largely useless sagebrush oceans. There was, along the Rio Grande, a nice richness of grass most years.

Rising above all this, from El Paso north beyond Taos were mountain ranges, many of them in the south raw and jagged like carnivorous teeth, in the north softer and covered with the dark carpets of evergreen trees and, in autumn, the golden leaves of white-trunked aspens.

Regardless of its relatively lush spots, the Spaniards found the entire realm a harsh and disappointing place, a nightmare of extreme cold and heat, of dust, and soil that required elaborate irrigation channels to be of any use at all (but very fertile once watered amply). Life for the colonists would be arduous, occasionally life threatening, and mostly boring.

## *Spanish Rule*

In this large and unpromising territory, Oñate established seven missionary districts and appointed a civilian *alcalde,* or leader, for each. The colonists were told to settle lands for their farms and herds apart and away from the pueblos. Christianizing and civilizing the Pueblos was to be the exclusive work of the friars, who were to move into the pueblos and persuade the Indians to help build mission churches.

Imperial traditions, in place for almost a century of Spanish expansion, included two major ways in which certain leading members of a colony could require the labor of the "pacified" Indians. One called *encomienda* specified that in return for deeds of exceptional value to the Crown (usually military), certain colonists were awarded the right to collect tribute from specified portions of the native populations, having a certain reciprocal role of guardianship over them, as well as being obliged to supply military aid to the provincial governors. This was, of course, a feudal holdover, but much of what was available in terms of institutions, ideals, and culture in the Spanish New World was medieval rather than anything new arising from Renaissance enlightenment in far-off Europe. And, to be sure, Spain itself was highly resistant to the new ideas and technical progress of what came to be called the Renaissance.

The other institution was *repartimiento*, by which Indians were drafted by the civil authorities to build those projects the governor deemed necessary. The Indians were to be paid a fair wage and their term of labor was to be limited. The government back in Spain was quite specific about these systems, setting various firm limits so that the Indians would not be abused. But enforcing limits on a new frontier months away from New Spain, much less Spain itself, could of course be difficult if not impossible to carry out.

The Spanish Crown, in other words, had authorized what seemed to be a relatively benign system for ruling natives in the far-flung colonial realms, but there were weak *Spanish helmet*

seams, as it were, in the system. One was enforcement. The other was a certain tension set up between the secular leaders and the religious. In repartimiento, the colonists had to pay for the services of the Indians. The friars, on the other hand, did not have to pay the Indians for their work at the missions. Future quarrels were, in essence, built into the system.

However, before any such troubles broke out, and before all but a couple Franciscans had repaired to their missionary districts with the civilian alcaldes (mayors, sort of), another kind of trouble exploded in the form of the colonists' first bone-chilling winter.

Many of the early Spanish accounts, by the way, speak of the terrible cold of the New Mexico winters, and lately historians have pointed out that the northern hemisphere was at that time in the throes of what is called the Little Ice Age, which lasted into the nineteenth century.

This climatic reversal has explained a great number of historical events, one of the least important being people skating on the Thames in England, which is no longer feasible. Thus, it has been claimed by historians, the settlements along the Rio Grande would have been much colder than today. But I found a recent report by Craig E. Allen, an ecologist with the U.S. Geological Survey, who found that various typical southwestern plants have the same ranges today as three centuries ago. This means that temperatures (and rainfall) were much the same then as now. The Little Ice Age appears to have not reached New Mexico.

On the other hand, the eruption of Huaynaputina, a Peruvian volcano, in 1600 evidently wrought havoc in the following year and has been implicated in such temporary weather effects as the worst harvest ever known till then in Russia. Large volcanic eruptions have the effect, usually, of cooling the climate briefly. Whatever the temporary effects of the volcano on the climate of New Mexico, the cold in New Mexico was surely worse than anything the Spanish had encountered far to the south in subtropical New Spain.

## *Violence at Acoma*

In late October, 1598, Oñate headed west with a sizable party to obtain the allegiance of the westernmost pueblos—Acoma, Zuni, and the Hopi villages— and to look for a passage to the South Sea, which the Spanish believed was not far off. A month later Oñate's nephew, Juan de Zaldívar, led a smaller group to join up with his uncle. Zaldívar's party reached the base of a huge, craggy, 400-foot-high mesa, a vast rocky headland on which the pueblo of Acoma sat, an impregnable place that had been inhabited for at least three or four hundred years and perhaps more.

One rocky and nearly vertical trail led to the top, and from there one looked out at a forbidding landscape dropped onto the earth by an angry god. Here lay badlands, *malpaís,* where the black blood of volcanoes had coagulated over the land. Yet, in the valley immediately below Acoma there were farms that in good years produced a plenitude of corn, beans, and squash.

Zaldívar's party called up from below, asking for provisions for their trip west. This was not an opportune moment for such a request. Back in San Juan, the local native people were already feeling put upon by the Spanish demands for food, and many Pueblos shared the feeling. The Acomas, after protesting, finally agreed to accommodate the Spaniards. On December 4, 1598, Zaldívar and a handful of his men clambered up the rugged trail, all set to buy firewood and corn for the men and their horses down below.

While the Spaniards bargained in several different groups, suddenly a great cry went up, and the Acomas attacked. When the violence subsided, Zaldívar and twelve other Spaniards were dead. A handful had vaulted over the side of the great sandstone fortress, two of them surviving the fall in a (luckily) sandy area. No one knows what set the violence off for sure, but the most plausible explanation, arrived at in later court hearings, was that one of Zaldívar's men snatched one of the many domesticated turkeys that also inhabited the lofty pueblo, and its owner, a woman, screamed. What the soldier could not have known was that the plentiful turkeys were not just a source of food and of feathers for cloaks. They were very much part of the spiritual and ceremonial heart of the Acoma culture. Snatching one unceremoniously would be seen as an egregious sacrilege.

Once informed of this massacre, the grief-stricken and infuriated Don Juan de Oñate presumed it was a deliberate plot. He and his force returned to the Río Bravo del Norte and the pueblo of Santo Domingo, where he questioned the Spanish survivors and others, seeking the friars' agreement that a severe punishment was justified, lest the rest of the estimated sixty thousand Pueblos (a nearly absurd exaggeration) rise up and slaughter the colonists and their military protectors.

Zaldívar's brother, Vincente de Zaldívar, led seventy men back to Acoma, arriving on January 21, 1599. Using the precipitous trail up the mesa, they proceeded to overwhelm the Acomas by force of superior arms including swords, knives, and the fearsome harquebuses, destroying the pueblo, burning much of it to the ground, killing about eight hundred people (it was estimated, perhaps a bit wildly), and herding some seventy men and five hundred women and children back to the Río del Norte and upstream to the pueblo of Santo Domingo, where the captives were to be tried. Santo Domingo was the religious capital of the colony, the seat of the Franciscan enterprise, and Oñate sought the approval of the clergy for such an important matter.

The justice the Spanish are said to have meted out seems to twenty-first century sensibilities to be diabolically harsh. But these were far harsher times and the friars agreed with Oñate that severe punishment met the criteria of justice: it would help protect the innocent, restore stolen goods, punish the transgressors, and preserve the peace. According to the Spanish, the Acomas, whether they knew it or not, had committed a capital crime in attacking the representatives of the Spanish Crown. The survivors received what was not totally unconventional treatment by seventeenth-century Spanish standards. Since execution was a standard sentence for such treasonous acts, Oñate could claim to have been relatively lenient.

As Oñate wrote and read to the assembled Spaniards and prisoners and the other Pueblos at Santo Domingo:

> To twenty year of servitude I am obliged to condemn and do condemn all the male and female Indians of the aforementioned pueblo who are prisoners. The Indian men of twenty-five years or more are to have one foot cut off and twenty years of personal service.
>
> The Indian men of less than twenty-five years down to twelve, I likewise condemn to twenty years of personal service.
>
> The Indian women of twelve years or more, I likewise condemn to twenty years of personal service.
>
> Two Indians from the province of Moqui [Hopi] who were present and fought in the aforementioned pueblo of Acoma and were apprehended, I sentence to have their right hands cut off and to be set free, so that they make known in their land the punishment given them.
>
> All the boys and girls of twelve years and younger, I declare to be free as [they are] innocent of the grave crime for which I punish their parents. And because of my obligation to demonstrate royal shelter, patronage, and protection for the aforementioned boys and girls, I leave all of the girls of twelve years or less to the disposition of our *padre comisario*, Fray Alonso Martínez, in order that a person so qualified and Christian as he might assign and place them in monasteries and situations, within and outside this realm, where he thinks they may acquire understanding of Our Lord God and salvation of their souls.[5]

Oñate went on to leave the disposition of the boys to his *sargento mayor*, and ordered that the old people who were "too decrepit to fight" be exiled to live among the surrounding Apaches. Some disagreement exists among historians as to whether the dismemberments were actually carried out. A noted historian of the Southwest, John L. Kessell, has been quoted as saying there is no documentary evidence that they were. But in the document translated above by the Hopi Documentary History Project (an ongoing study started in 2000 by the Arizona State Museum), several paragraphs are appended and signed by Spanish officers, testifying that Oñate actually did write this and read it out loud "*verbum ad verbum*" on February 12, 1598. One other paragraph, also certified by the official secretary, says that the "aforementioned sentence was executed and discharged, exactly as directed, in the aforementioned pueblo of Santo Domingo, and in other pueblos in the immediate area, [where] on different days the Indians' feet and hands were cut off."

It stands to reason. This, as noted, was a common punishment in those days, practiced in the Jamestown colony by the English a decade or so after the Acoma massacre.

Long before the twenty years of servitude had been completed, however, Acoma would be repopulated and the pueblo rebuilt, presumably in part by escaped slaves. But for now, the word went out throughout the eighty-seven thousand square miles that it had taken only half of the Spanish soldiers present in the region three days to defeat the Acomas in their towering and heretofore impregnable fortress. The power of their weapons would now be universally feared. The loss of such a renowned stronghold was a psychological blow not unlike the Spanish loss of their armada.

## Discouraging Prospects

Within a few months of the establishment of the colony of New Mexico, life was in almost total disarray. It is almost impossible to imagine how disgusted the entire complement of Spanish was—soldiers, colonists, and friars. For these people were familiar with the stories (at least) of fabulous Aztec riches, of shiploads of silver sent back to Spain, of well-behaved Indians working the mines, caring for households. The New Spain they had all left was a relatively civilized place, orderly, promising. But it took only a few months to demonstrate that attempting a colony in this forgotten remote place was a terrible mistake, a calamity unfolding.

More than half the Spanish soldiers and most of the colonists were in a rebellious mood, plotting to return to New Spain despite the laws that made such an abandonment treasonous. They were totally discouraged by failure to find any rich mines, not to mention that they were forbidden from using agricultural lands already in use by the Indians, which was practically all of the best agricultural lands from Socorro to Taos. The colonists who didn't huddle in the existing buildings in San Juan pueblo lived in rude buildings quickly thrown up against the cold. They were afflicted by the cold, bedbugs, and vermin. Everyone was afflicted by head lice, according to the indefatigable historian of daily life in Spanish New Mexico, Marc Simmons. They had arrived in New Mexico too late to plant any crops and it appeared that they might well all starve. They lived in constant fear that some among the overwhelming numbers of Pueblos might decide to take vengeance on them for what the Spanish soldiers had done at Acoma. One of the friars, described as more than seventy years old, Fray Francisco de San Miguel, complained that "we cannot preach the Gospel now, for it is despised by these people on account of our great offenses and harm we have done them."

In this first winter, Oñate's soldiers forcefully took rations, blankets, and women from the pueblos, leaving many of them totally destitute. Soon after, in the Tompiro pueblos to the south, the inhabitants refused to meet the Spanish demands for food, blankets, and other supplies. Retribution was quick. The soldiers set fire to parts of the pueblos, killed several Indians as they fled, and subsequently hanged two leaders and an interpreter.

Meanwhile, Oñate seemed to have lost interest in New Mexico, and spent a good deal of his time traveling (with a complement of soldiers) out to the plains in quest of the chimerical gold of Quivira. Later, he continued west as far as the Gulf of California in quest of the legendary passage to the Pacific. On returning to San Gabriel from his fruitless journey, Oñate found the capital nearly deserted. Most of the colonists and all but two Franciscans had fled, convinced that they or the Indians or both would all starve to death.

Oñate and the colonists were unaware of the famine and plague that wiped out half a million people in the Spanish kingdoms of Castile and Andalusia that year and the next, 1600. By this time, growth of Spain's population had stagnated, while the mercantile economies of Europe depended in part on population growth. Losing a half-million people was a calamity, and just as New Mexico was unraveling, so too the Spanish Empire was in need of major reworking.

By 1605, Oñate was essentially bankrupted by the costs of the New Mexico enterprise (the expenses of which, except for the Crown-financed Franciscan efforts, cost him in the end some six hundred thousand pesos, a fortune). Meanwhile, the Viceroy of New Spain was convinced that the New Mexico colony—"this worthless land," he called it—should be given up and, worse, the King of Spain was calling for Oñate to be replaced and his mismanagement investigated. What finally saved the New Mexico colony from extinction within a decade of its founding was the realization by the Crown that were the Spanish to leave, the Natives who had converted to Christianity would be abandoned to who knew what fate among the barbarians. And the friars claimed more than seven thousand such conversions, a happily inflated figure, which, it seems, they pulled from a hat.

So King Philip III, though his treasury was in terrible shape, took on the expense of continuing this unpromising experiment. New Mexico had been saved by the friars, and its founder, like many other governors who would follow, was ruined. The friars would now have the upper hand, they were sure, since the government had proclaimed New Mexico a vineyard of the Lord.

Banished forever from New Mexico, Oñate, unlike many disgraced successors, would bounce back, making his way to Spain where he was eventually made an officer of the royal court and commissioned to be the inspector of the royal mines.

# CHAPTER 4

# The Pueblo World

JUST WHO WERE THE NATIVE AMERICANS into whose land and lives the Spanish had come? The Spanish had no idea. Where they had come from, how long they had lived in these arid lands, and what sort of worldview they held—these were evidently not of much interest to the friars or the secular administrators. The colonists were under orders to remain distant from the Pueblo people as well as the pueblos. It is safe to assume these august rules were ignored often, producing a goodly number of mixed couples even early on.

The Pueblos knew precisely where they had come from, and where they had sojourned before coming to the present locations. They had come from previous worlds, as many as three previous worlds, emerging through a now sacred place in the ground into this world of today and of recent history. They were unlikely to discuss this and other matters about their beliefs and lifeways with the Franciscans. As mythologist David Leeming noted in describing the fundamental mythological stories of the Pueblo people, the ceremonial practices of nearly all the Pueblo people "are to some extent secret to this day. Even the myths we have are somewhat suspect, as they are not necessarily told to non-Indians with any consistency, perhaps to preserve at least an aspect of secrecy."[6]

The main exception to all of this secrecy is the Hopi people. At least some Hopis have been far more forthcoming than the more private Pueblos who look askance at how open the Hopis have been in explaining such things as their creation myth and the multiple meanings promoted in a katsina dance. (Mythology, by the way, is another word, partly pejorative, for other peoples' religious beliefs. To many who don't subscribe to it, for example, the Bible is simply the mythology of the Jews and Christians.) But we do know that most of the Pueblos—Taos and Picuris may be exceptions—share the basic emergence story from earlier worlds. And from the Hopis, we have a story of what happened that is agreed to in essence by most of the often-argumentative Hopi people. It is adapted here by my wife and me from longer and more detailed versions, and approved by some Hopi readers.

*In the beginning there was endless space in which nothing existed but Tawa, the sun spirit, who contrived to gather some of the elements of space and inject some of his own substance into them and thereby created the First World, inhabited by insect-like creatures who lived in caves and fought among themselves. Dissatisfied, Tawa sent a new spirit, Spider Grandmother, down to prepare them for a long trip. She led them on a long journey during which they changed form, grew fur on their bodies, acquired tails, and took on the shape of dogs, wolves, and bears.*

*They arrived in the Second World, but Tawa was still displeased because these creatures did not understand the meaning of life. So Spider Grandmother was dispatched again, and while she led them on their second journey, Tawa created a Third World, lighter and moist. By the time they had arrived in the Third World, they had become people. Spider Grandmother cautioned them to renounce evil and live in harmony.*

*They built villages and planted corn, but it was cold. Again Spider Grandmother arrived; she taught them to weave and make pots. But the pots could not be baked, and the corn did not grow well because of the chill.*

*One day a hummingbird arrived, explaining that he had been sent by Masauwu, who lived in yet another world above the sky, called the Upper World. Masauwu was the owner of fire and caretaker of the place of the dead. The hummingbird taught the people to make fire with a drill. Then he left.*

*They learned to bake their pottery so it wouldn't break. They warmed their fields by lighting fires. They cooked their meat instead of eating it raw. Things were better in the Third World now.*

*But sorcerers began to unleash evil into the world, making medicines that would turn their minds from virtue. Men gambled instead of tending their fields. Women revolted. Rains failed to come, and the corn failed.*

*Spider Grandmother came again to warn them, telling the people who still had good hearts that they should leave this world and go to the upper world. A chief and his wise men prayed for four days and then, out of clay and by performing a special ceremony, they created a swallow and asked it to find a way to the Upper World. The swallow flew high up into the sky and found an opening, but strong winds buffeted it and it flew back.*

*The chief and the wise men made a dove, and it flew through the opening and found a great land spreading in all directions but with no life on it. The dove flew back and reported.*

*This time the men made a hawk, and it flew up, only to return with the same message. Finally, a catbird flew through the opening and came upon Masauwu, who said the people could come. Hearing this message, the people were elated. Then they realized they had no way to climb up to the opening. Spider Grandmother reminded them of the chipmunk, who lived on pine nuts and might help them plant a tall tree.*

*They enlisted Chipmunk. He planted a spruce, but it didn't grow tall enough. Then he tried a fir pine, but it grew only slightly higher. A long-needled pine also failed. The chipmunk asked if someone with an evil heart was present, and the people assured him of their pure intentions. The fourth time a bamboo reed was tried, and Spider Grandmother told the people to sing so it would grow high. Eventually it succeeded in growing through the opening. This was the* sipapuni, *and Chipmunk explained that the people could climb up through the hollow reed and through the sipapuni.*

*The chief and the wise men drew four lines in the ground and said if any sorcerers crossed the lines they would perish. Then, led by Spider Grandmother and her twin sons, the people climbed up the reed into the upper world, the Fourth World of the Hopis.*[7]

The Hopis' *sipapuni* is located at the confluence of the Little Colorado River and the Colorado River, a place deep in Grand Canyon. Another sipapuni, that of the Sandia people, lies somewhere high in the Sandia Mountains above present-day Albuquerque. All or most of the Pueblo people emerged from earlier worlds after some experiences that sound not unlike a process of evolution, and then their migrations in this world began.

Elsewhere in North America, the most common creation story involves a hero, often in the form of an animal, who dives down from a celestial perch into the murky waters below to collect mud and bring it back up to form the earth upon which we all now walk. The Southwestern tribes are extremely different from those elsewhere. For example, there is nothing like the *katsinas* anywhere else on the continent.

That something like the Hopi creation story told here was told three hundred or so years ago is fairly certain. It almost surely was a story told at

Chaco Canyon and Mesa Verde, monumental stone buildings inhabited by people who were thought to have vanished altogether from the planet around AD 1300 but who have now been shown to be ancestors to the Hopis and Pueblo people. Whatever conditions led to the abandonment of these structures (the reasons run from religious overkill to drought and even cannibalism by invaders), it was time to find new places, new lives, but the old stories surely persisted in one recognizable form or another. The Pueblos have done a lot of moving and their stories have been part of what they brought with them, along with the ability to grow corn, squash, and beans.

The Spaniards soon learned that the Indians spoke different languages, but in many superficial (meaning noticeable) ways they were very similar, especially if the outliers—Taos and Picuris in the northeast, and Hopi and Zuni in the northwest—were not counted. The Hopi language, for example, is part of a family of languages called Uto-Aztecan. The Utes and Shoshones northeast of Hopi and the Aztecs far to the south shared this language group. On the other hand, the Zuni language is a complete puzzle to linguists: it does not appear to be in any way related to any other language in North America (or anywhere else).

It is not unreasonable that the conquistadors and the friars, arriving in the pueblo world with little knowledge of the native people, looked upon these new wards of the Crown as all the same. They all lived in relatively small villages, though the Spaniards would have noticed that the littlest ones were in the south and the largest in the north—in terms of inhabitants and the number of stories of the pueblos. Today, the main Taos pueblo is the largest such structure left, rising four stories high. All the other pueblos and Hopi villages have now reverted to one-story buildings, with rare buildings of two stories.

The Spaniards noted that all the Pueblos farmed, growing the same crops—maize, beans, and squash along with native cotton and various tobacco-like plants. They hunted animals, from rabbits to deer and pronghorns, and gathered wild plants for healing and ceremonial use. They dressed in much the same way (or didn't dress, by Spanish standards), typically wearing only cotton kilts and moccasins of deerskin. Nakedness was apparently not uncommon, in season of course.

They made baskets, pots, and turquoise "baubles." And they often held costumed and masked dances—in the dusty plazas formed by their homes—that were perceived as either a form of devil worship or foolish folk dances, but nothing that could be seen by civilized people as anything like kneeling before the Cross.

Where did they come from? Here in this world, the Pueblo people knew they came from the four directions, on foot. They had once lived in the mountains in the south in Mexico, in the southwestern desert crisscrossed by canals now gone dry, from the great houses built exquisitely from finely crafted stone and then abandoned. They came from the red canyonlands of today's Utah, from the buffalo plains to the east, and from the Rockies in the north. Over the millennia they came for a multiplicity of reasons. They spoke many languages and carried with them ancient traditions that grew and changed, becoming partly new rites and ceremonies as needed to render new conditions habitable.

Most of them had been agriculturalists for a thousand years or more, mostly living as extended families, and they became villagers, needing to invent new social means of dealing with the complex strains and benefits of extended village life. From their west, arriving in their midst to assist in these new requirements, came the spirits they would call *katsinas*. These were nature spirits, and they could take the form of clouds. They were ancestors, returning in any form of moisture, be it a drop of water on a leaf, or a winter snowfall, even the moisture at the corners of a laughing mouth. They could become embodied and dance in the village plazas, where they were asked to intervene with other spirits to send timely rains to the fields. The katsinas joined the riverless Hopis, the westernmost of these people, and danced among all the other pueblos east of the Hopi mesas except the plains-oriented pueblos of Picuris and Taos.

By the time the Spanish arrived in their midst, the Pueblos had been in place for three hundred or more years. The Hopis, driven by prophecies to stop their wandering when they saw a great star overhead in daylight, say the first of their clans arrived in 1066, the year of the supernova noted by the Chinese. Archaeologists are yet to confirm this, not that it matters to the Hopi. Tradi-tion holds that there soon arose a squabble between two brothers in the first Hopi village, one of them leaving that village to form another called Oraibi, one of three candidates for the oldest continuously inhabited place in the United States. The other two candidates are Acoma and Taos.

Most of the Pueblo people have strong historical memories of places where they sojourned for a time before arriving in their present places (see map at front of book). One of the best ways to learn all the initially confusing pueblo and language names on the map is to use a simile by Alfonso Ortiz, a twentieth-century Tewa anthropologist. He wrote of "the villages of adobe and stone that, for the most part, are strung along the Rio Grande and its tributaries like beads upon a crooked string." More than a crooked string, the array resembles something like a bush, with all the beads located on tributaries to the main string. And of course there are a few outliers—beads that still rest on the table rather than having been strung. These are Pecos far to the east, and the far western peoples, Zuni and Hopi.

One of the more confusing matters is that among all the Pueblo people are seven separate spoken languages, and on the map the groupings of the languages are indicated in gray. To extend the use of Dr. Ortiz's simile, the separate language groups can be thought of as different colors of beads. There are Tiwa-colored pueblos of Taos and Picuris in the far north. Also, there are Tiwa-colored beads, including Sandia and Isleta, around the area of present-day Albuquerque where Coronado stayed for a few destructive months.

South of Taos and Picuris are the Tewa-colored beads in a kind of orderly clump along the Rio Grande.

To their northwest are the several Towa-speaking beads of Jemez (pronounced Hay-miss), and far to the east is the Towa-speaking bead of Pecos.

A bit to the south of the Jemez and Tewa beads are several Keresan-colored beads of Cochiti, Zia, Santa Ana, Santo Domingo, and San Felipe. To their west, across the Rio Grande, is another Keres-colored bead, Acoma, that lies off the string.

And so on.

The aptness of Ortiz' comparison lies, poetically, in the fact that the Pueblo people adorned themselves with necklaces and earrings of shell and turquoise beads from the earliest of times, beginning two thousand years ago when they lived elsewhere in the Southwest. One of the unique features of the Pueblo people is that they are among the very few Native Americans who can trace their existence directly back with clearly unbroken cultural continuity two millennia spent in the same part of the world.

The people of Taos and Picuris and the Tiwa-speaking people to the south came to this part of the world from the plains. Just how the Tiwa Pueblos in the south and two in the north wound up separated by more than a hundred miles is anybody's guess. It could have been a political or religious dispute, or something more benign that sent some of the people south at an unknown point in time.

The people of Cochiti and Santo Domingo and the other Keresan-speaking Pueblos arrived only after a sojourn in present-day Bandolier National Monument, living in the white cliffs in the Jemez Mountains in northern New Mexico. Bandolier was created when an ancient volcanic eruption covered the land with a titanic amount of ash that subsequently hardened into rock.

No one knows for sure where the southern Pueblo people came from—the Piros and Tompiros—because they eventually ceased to exist as a tribe, along with many other Pueblos including those to the east (except for Pecos which was abandoned much later).

The Tewa-speaking Pueblos, including those from Tesuque where Fray Pío was murdered, migrated over time down the Rio Grande and the Rio Chama from southeastern Colorado, forming numerous villages that eventually combined into the seven Tewa pueblos of historic times.

Meanwhile, Towa-speaking Pecos, which lay on the eastern edge of pueblo country, and the Towa-speaking Jemez (now consolidated into one village) evidently became mountain dwellers early on.

To the west of the Rio Grande lies Acoma, another Keresan pueblo that is older than the others. Also west were the Zuni pueblos first visited by the appalling Estéban.

Farthest west were the Hopi mesas, with five main villages when the Spanish arrived, all speaking different but mutually intelligible dialects of the Hopi language. According to Hopi history, they became one people after various groups assembled at the present spot from all of the four cardinal directions, a series of events called the Gathering of the Clans.

The pueblo lands, with at least seven distinct languages, were surrounded in virtually all directions by bands of what came to be called Apaches who often visited the pueblos either peacefully or hostilely. The Apaches were chiefly hunters and gatherers who had arrived in the region a century or so before the Spanish. Over an unknown period of time, they had made the stunningly long trek south from the Yukon-Northwest Territories region of Canada and spoke the language of their fellow Athabaskans who had elected to stay put. They filled in the empty, arid space around the pueblo lands, raiding, trading, and being a source of continuing consternation for the Pueblo people. The pueblos were occasionally raided by Utes, in addition to the Apaches, descending on them from what is now southern Colorado.

## Common Threads

For all their differences, the Pueblo people shared a recognizably similar architecture—adobe (mud brick) buildings rising as high as seven stories in some cases, surrounding a plaza, or several plazas. The Hopis, however, having extremely limited water supplies, used only stone for building. The rooms in these multi-storied buildings were usually rectangular and entered not through doors but by ladders through holes in the flat roofs, just as Coronado discovered at Hawikuh. Each pueblo had one or more underground rooms called *kivas*, which were devoted chiefly to ceremonial use and also entered by ladder from the roof. Kivas were typically round, but in the Hopi villages they were rectangular. The kivas, dating to much earlier times in places like the Ancestral Puebloan great houses, were where katsinas danced in winter and where men of various religious societies gathered to smoke, pray, and plan throughout the year.

The ceremonial fires that burned in the kivas created smoke that drifted out the entrance on the roof, and gave rise to the derogatory Spanish name for them: *estufas*, meaning stoves. For the Indians, smoke carried prayers to the world of spirits. The kivas found in the large and small buildings of the Chaco culture have a small hole in the floor, as do today's kivas. Today the hole is thought to ceremonially represent the sipapuni, and it probably did so seven hundred years ago.

The Pueblos were focused on growing their staples—corn, squash, and beans—and keeping enough from any given year's crop to maintain a two- or three-year supply in storage rooms in the pueblo. Some of the Pueblos also encouraged the growth of a natural cotton, which was woven into shawls and other clothing. In addition to traditional crafts that they made, they also traded for shells, copper ornaments and bells, and macaw feathers in return for turquoise, which was plentiful in New Mexico and Arizona. The desired trade goods came from Mexico and farther south along trade routes that had been used for centuries if not millennia. The Pueblos also traded crops for meat and skins with the surrounding Apaches and other Native people beyond.

Culturally the pueblos had much in common—a reliance on communal effort rather than individual achievement. If any individuals tried to rise above the group in some disapproved way, they risked "being witched"— becoming inexplicably ill or dying. The Pueblo people all had coherent world views infused in virtually every detail of their lives and were guided by a profoundly complex spiritual sense of the universe and their place in it. The steadfast adherence in most of the pueblos to their cultural heritage, and the cooperative spirit in which they joined together in the twentieth century to protect their ways of life, has led to the notion that they were always from time immemorial dutiful, peaceful people who produced a kind of polyglot

Eden along the Rio Grande.

However, pictographs and petroglyphs in the region, ubiquitous rock carvings of spirals, animal and human figures, and shields (thousands of round shields) indicate that—beginning in about AD 1500 with the newly arrived Apaches and the more distant and northerly Utes—they were often at war with each other over ancient gripes, thefts, and whatnot. Most Pueblos were led by deeply religious older men who looked after spiritual matters, without which there could be no proper internal social order and peace. War chiefs and other officials dealt with secular matters, such as tribal conflicts or lesser disputes.

A great variety of social structures—clans, for example, with traditional ceremonial chores and special knowledge that benefited everyone—held the people together against the centrifugal forces at play in all human societies. Many of the Rio Grande pueblos without a clan system were split into summer and winter halves—tribal divisions called *moieties* by anthropologists—alternating governance of the pueblo every six months. With different names from pueblo to pueblo, they typically were in charge either for the six winter months or the six summer months. Almost all of the pueblos were home to medicine societies and a variety of secret societies that held esoteric rites on behalf of the general welfare. All of these components of pueblo society were held together—or not, as the case might be—by the religious leader of the time. This position was sometimes inherited, at least by clan membership (as with the Bear Clan of the Hopis), but sometimes by other means of appointment.

The Spanish thought—at first at least—that the Pueblos were good-natured, hard-working, and thrifty folk, and may well have taken them to be simple, if not simple-minded. It would take far more than a century and a great loss of life before the Spanish realized how astonishingly rich, sophisticated, and deep-rooted were the cultures they had determined early on to eradicate. Indeed, it would be well into the twentieth century before outsiders would gain any real appreciation for these distinctive ways of life in at least some of the less private pueblos.

At the outset, however, the Spanish were surprised by the exceptional cleanliness of the pueblos. Accustomed to simply throwing garbage and sewage out of the house into the streets, they found that the Pueblos kept chamber pots on the roofs, which were emptied in the morning far away from the pueblo proper, often in the fields as fertilizer. The pueblo world was certainly dusty, but houses were typically immaculately swept. Typhus, that frequent

*Hopi rock art. Churches and a Spanish ship?*
*Hopis say they are all stars.*

scourge of townsfolk, was never known to be a problem among the pueblos.

Women's roles were specific, and in their sphere—typically the household—the women were unquestioned and powerful. Men chiefly tended the fields that lay outside of the pueblo, but apparently it was women who, before the arrival of the Apaches, had done the farming, while men went off hunting. But with the arrival of raiders determined to carry off Pueblo women as slaves, and with women being too important to lose, men took over being exposed in the fields. Women raised the children and engaged in pottery, basket making, and other chores, providing the family with most of the implements needed in the course of daily life. Among today's pueblos, there are some in which status is conferred by birth, but it is not known when this arose. It could be very ancient, or it could have become an issue at some point with the continuing intermarriage of Pueblo people with Hispanics and others after the arrival of the Spanish.

Ceremonial and ritual life required a great deal of time, including rehearsals for katsina dances and other requirements. Medicine men and women spent much time out in the surrounding lands and up in the mountains, collecting medicinal plants. Hopis, for example, had to go a hundred miles to gather evergreen boughs the katsinas wore around their necks. Women's rituals and men's rituals were probably separate for the most part and mostly secret. It is possible that many of these secret rituals were never known to, or even guessed at by, the Franciscans. It was the katsina dances and other ceremonies that took place in the plazas that attracted their notice and their enduring hatred.

The deepest that most Spanish friars and others would eventually probe the pueblo culture was to try to perceive analogues. For example, the Sun, evidently a single main deity, could be taken to be the pueblo version of God, with the katsinas being something akin to angels. Such similarities may, in individual circumstances, have led to some sort of accommodation in a few instances. (Condescension is of course preferable to extermination.) But for the most part, it was the katsinas who the Spanish believed to be the Devil's spawn.

On the other hand, in 1972, Vincent Scully, a Yale professor of art history, produced a lavishly illustrated tome called *Pueblo: Mountain, Village, Dance,* in which he pronounced the pueblo katsina dances to be the most profound works of art ever created in North America. It was these dances and what the Spaniards, especially the Franciscans, thought they represented, that stuck so hatefully in the Spanish craw and which they felt needed to be stopped. For the Indians, the dances were not only spiritual affairs of the utmost importance but also a life-affirming and life-giving mode by which the Pueblo people engineered their lands to be fecund. Without the katsina dances, the world would soon become a dismal place, unfit for life. The invaders did not come to understand the profound role of the katsina dances and never described them in much detail because they were thought to be satanic. To write of them in detail, for example, or to sit in the plaza and watch them, was to invite into one's neighborhood the malevolent powers of the Devil.

## *The Hopi Katsina Dance*

Currently, sometimes (and only in some villages) non-Indians are welcome to attend the dances, the belief being that the more prayers the better. Unfortunately, sometimes a village is disappointed by disrespectful behavior at the dances by non-Natives, so they close them to outsiders. No non-Native gets to see a Rio Grande Pueblo katsina dance. In Santo Domingo pueblo today, women and girls are not allowed to look upon a katsina or even a representation of one. On one occasion, some Pueblo leaders asked the Museum of Indian Culture and Arts in Santa Fe not to include a particular photograph in their exhibition of my wife Susanne's photographs of Hopis and Navajos. The reason: there was a katsina *doll* behind the subject's shoulder and the museum did not want many women to be excluded from the exhibit hall. (Of course, Susanne replaced the photograph with another.)

What follows is a description of a summer Hopi katsina dance, which takes place in the plaza in daylight. The late winter and early spring dances take place in a kiva at night. A week or so after the summer solstice, the katsinas leave the villages for six months during which time they dwell in San Francisco Peaks, the remains of a great volcano visible from most of the villages a hundred or so miles west on the horizon near Flagstaff. There, until the sun starts back to its summer house at winter solstice, the katsinas rehearse the bringing of rain and in December, timed by the moon, as is the entire annual ceremonial cycle, the katsinas return to the villages with copious amounts of bean sprouts miraculously grown in the dead of winter. No one can grow beans in the cold and dark—except the katsinas.

**Behold:** This day, the sacred mountain, the San Francisco Peaks, rises blue above the far horizon in the west, a few wispy clouds near the summit. The huge bowl of sky is otherwise cloudless and the sun has been awake for four hours. Women, young and old, wearing cotton shawls, sit on stone *bancos* around the edge of the dusty plaza in this village high on a yellow sandstone mesa. To the south, a day's run across the nearly featureless land, improbable shapes rise on the horizon, buttes, one of them in the form of a human breast the Hopis teasingly call "The Tit." Naked children dart in and out of the shadows and sunlight in the plaza. Some of the older girls and boys stand on the flat rooftops of the yellow stone buildings in the thin dry air some six hundred feet above the desert and the cornfields down on the dry lands below.

A delicious tension begins to animate the audience and soon, from beyond the plaza, a loud hoot is heard, and the sound of a gourd rattle, and then forty similarly arrayed katsinas file into the plaza, tended by one of the village's elders, the katsina father who sprinkles the katsinas with corn meal—spirit food. The dancers wear buckskin moccasins, necklaces of spruce boughs from the sacred mountain, and white cotton kilts. Bronze bodies are streaked with earthy colors—ochres, reds, yellows—with multicolored beaked faces, eyes glittering from horizontal slits. They sing, a low chanting like a deep distant wind, while a drum thumps assertively, metronomically adjusting the observers' pulses. Fox tails sway behind the kilts, turtle shells fixed to the katsinas' calves go *plok-plok,* and copper bells from Mexico go *chink-ch-chink* on the stomping legs as the spirits dance this way, pause, turn, dance that way, back and forth, over and over, brightly painted gourd rattles in hand, complementing the relentless drumbeat.

All day in the hot sun, punctuated by short breaks, the spirits dance and as the solemn performance wears on, the plaza is filled with hope, promise, generosity, and prayer. The spirits sing a special poetry, phrases and words not used in regular day-to-day conversation, songs that have been passed down for unknown numbers of generations. They sing of the proper way to be a Hopi.

The katsinas like to dance, and the Hopis have welcomed them, provided a place to dance, and fed them. In turn, the katsina father enjoins them to arrange for rains to come. These dances are a matter not of pleas but of a proper reciprocity.

Clouds build up over San Francisco Peaks and break off, hastening tantalizingly toward the Hopi mesas and the cornfields in dry washes below, cornfields that will thrive only with a brief timely rain. Lavender shadows flow across the brown desert. In late afternoon the wind gusts up in the plaza; little clouds swirl and fall. The entire visible, audible world is a nearly infinite cathedral.

As the katsinas troop into the plaza after their last break, they carry baskets of food and wooden toys. Before they begin, they reach in their baskets and throw multicolored ears of corn—white, yellow, red, blue, representing the four directions—to the audience, and hand out simply carved, brightly colored dolls to the little girls and miniature bows and arrows to the little boys.

The next day begins the same way, the plaza filled with color, sound, physical action, and active prayer, but not long after the sun reaches the day's zenith, an ill-clad, dirty, and noisy band of ragamuffins descends headfirst down ladders from the surrounding houses. These are the clowns, called *tcuku*, which also means "to make a point," and they do things backward, upside down, wrong. For the rest of the day they will try to disrupt the profound formality of the katsinas, buffoonery and slapstick turning into outright ribaldry and the mimicking of bodily function. They become progressively degraded, acting out the corruption of humanity. They gossip, they fight, they covet things, and they accost people from the audience. They are gluttonous, greedy. They commit faux adultery, they projectile vomit, and they pretend to masturbate. The women in the audience love it, giggling, holding their shawls over their faces but peeking, clutching their sides. Laughter ripples out in competition with the solemn songs of the katsinas. At some point, the audience notices that an owl katsina has slipped into the plaza and is watching the clowns intently.

At the end of the day, the clowns succumb to the ultimate sin, the hubris of taunting, even imitating the katsinas. The owl katsina warns these ill-doers but they pay it no heed. Soon fierce whipper spirits go after the clowns, beating them with sharp-edged yucca whips, dousing them with mud, stuffing live snakes into their filthy clothes. Blood flows. Under the threat of death, the clowns repent.

And the world is back in order.

The katsina father directs the katsinas to go now and to bring rain to the Hopi fields down below, as they have generously done since before memory.

## *Age-Old Traditions*

More than likely, something similar to this took place regularly in the world of the pueblos in the time of the Spaniards four hundred years ago. And in even earlier times in Europe, an analog of this performance regularly used to occur. If one were able to attend the service at a cathedral in England in the year 1300 or 1400, for example, one would hear a Catholic mass not unrecognizable from one today (though in Latin), but one might also witness a play—a morality play about Everyman who journeys through the valley of sin and suffers greatly until he repents and is taken into the bosom of forgiveness. In New Mexico, in the time of the Spanish, no one saw the similarity.

# CHAPTER 5

# Saving Souls

IT WAS AN ASTONISHINGLY BOLD PLAN, one that only the very bravest of men would attempt to carry out. A handful of true believers, some fifty men of penitence with absolute loyalty to the Church, would walk singly on sandaled feet and unarmed into as many pueblos inhabited by approximately 60,000 pagan Native Americans (they calculated), and turn them into god-fearing Spaniards, overturning a way of life that, for all they knew, was hundreds of years old.

What one Franciscan wrote in 1584 to the Spanish King expressed the innocent hopes that appear in all mission statements of the time: "If your highness may be pleased to have the Holy Gospel preached to the people of those provinces with the necessary zeal, God our lord will be served and many idolatries and notable sins which the devil has implanted among the natives will be eradicated. Thus having succeeded in this holy purpose your royal crown will be served by an increase of vassals, tribute, and royal fifths."

To this end, the Viceroy appointed a new governor for New Mexico, which was now a royal province financed by the royal treasury. Pedro de Peralta arrived in 1610 with an additional group of friars and high hopes. At that time, there were some two hundred Spanish (or more accurately Hispanic) settlers centered near San Gabriel, many of them now staunch colonists determined to make something of themselves and their province. They were mostly *mestizos,* mixtures of Spanish and Mexican Indian bloodlines.

Many of the male colonists had imagined themselves rising in status, becoming *hidalgos,* addressed by the honorific word *don,* landowners with many cattle, sheep, and goats, with hired hands doing the herding and other ranch work while Native women helped out around the house. Such lives would eventually be attained by at least a few colonists, but in the early years the circumstances in which all the colonists labored and lived were poor.

In simple daily matters, New Mexico was unforgiving. Whatever clothes they brought with them (the governor, officers, and some colonists brought splendid finery, silks, and woolens) were soon all worn out due mainly to windblown dust. The colonists had to barter with the Indians for buckskins to make pants, shirts, skirts, moccasins, and any other kind of apparel.

Immediately after their arrival, the colonists set out to till what soil was available to them and plant a host of food plants brought from Spain and Mexico. These included wheat, barley, cabbage, onions, melons, and radishes, as well as tomatoes, chile, and new strains of corn. Orchard trees and grape vines came later. They discovered that the poor soil became fecund with the addition of water, as many necessary minerals existed in the near-desert soils. To irrigate, they dug networks of large and small ditches called *acequias*. They set up the institution of the *majordomo*, or ditch master. This was an office independent from any other political arm of the colony, a local man who parceled out the water to users, appointed people to help keep the ditches clear, and ran the water system with an iron hand. To this day, in many northern Rio Grande communities, the ditch master holds sway.

Plowing was done by oxen (usually two) pulling an awkward wooden plow, steadied by the farmer in its wake. Metal farm implements would come much later; wood was about the only useful material around. Heavy loads were pulled by two-wheeled wagons, clumsy, noisy, painfully slow, and prone to breaking down. The wheels were made of slabs of cottonwood trunks, rounded with chisels, and attached to a cottonwood axle. A mostly flat bottom and a wooden cage-like structure completed the vehicle, which was prone to wobbling back and forth as the axle wore down and to the breaking of wheels. These wagons would remain in service for another century in New Mexico, until wheels with metal rims came into wider use. It was basically the same design as carts used more than three thousand years ago in Asia and southern Europe, one of them dating back to 1400 BC.

Dogs—mostly mastiffs and greyhounds—were brought to New Mexico by the Spaniards, and soon interbred with smaller dogs that teemed in the pueblos, used there as alarms and for hunting. It is said by some that the pueblo dogs were also beloved pets, but I doubt that. Today, at Hopi and elsewhere on Indian lands, dogs are almost never allowed inside a house. The pueblo dogs were mostly feral and, as elsewhere around the world, served as a hedge against starvation. The settlers in New Mexico trained some of their dogs to herd sheep and goats, and a good herd dog was reputed to do the work of three men.

While the Spanish toolbox was extremely limited by modern standards, it dazzled the Pueblo and Apache people. Beads, knives, cloth, awls, scissors, mirrors—all these implements were eminently tradable and led to what is speculated to be the first major trade fairs in the region (though exactly when the first one occurred is not known). Settlers had these wonderful new implements to trade to both the Pueblo people and the Apaches (for pueblo corn and other produce, and for Apache meat and hides).

Regular trade fairs emerged where all the disparate groups of people got together peacefully to barter, but at first the settlers were forbidden by the Spanish leadership from attending them. The governor and his friends wanted to monopolize the trading, but the settlers complained so loudly to the Viceroy that he ordered the governor to let them attend. The Taos Fair in October of each year, after the harvest, became the most elaborate trade fair, and promised safe conduct for all who might otherwise be mutually hostile. More than trading took place; horse racing was popular, as were bouts of drinking. And as Marc Simmons points out, each year nine months later, in July, there was usually a larger than usual crop of new babies.

Except for these moments in the year, work was long and hard, and sources of entertainment few. It was a peasant's life for the most part. There were virtually no books in the province and most of the Spanish were illiterate. There was little to do besides working, drinking, playing cards, picking nits from one another's heads, and making love.

## *The Ordóñez Affair*

Governor Peralta came with a number of viceregal orders, one of which was to leave San Gabriel to the Pueblos and establish a more easily defended capital at Santa Fe where, in this era, there were no Native Americans.

For his first year or so, Peralta labored to get the new capital set up, including creating the *cabildo* (a kind of town board) for Santa Fe. The thirty-five *encomenderos* (those colonists who could exact special tribute from the Pueblos), were now required to maintain homes in the capital, and began hiring Pueblo laborers to build their houses there.

In late August of 1612, an ambitious and overbearing friar, Fray Isidro Ordóñez, arrived with twenty wagons and more Franciscans. He produced a letter, technically a patent, from the order's boss in New Spain (a Franciscan called the commissary general) putting Ordóñez in charge of the New Mexican *custodia* (meaning all the friars in the colony and their activities).

For unknown reasons, Ordóñez had developed an intense dislike for Governor Peralta and proceeded to make his life miserable. In Santa Fe, in an obvious power grab, the Franciscan insisted that Peralta announce that colonists were free to leave the colony whenever they pleased. Peralta refused. After all, this was a matter of established law in New Spain: it was illegal to abandon a colony. Ordóñez proceeded to make the announcement himself. Next he accused Peralta of underfeeding Pueblos engaged in public works in the new capital, and interfered with Peralta's men who were going to Taos to collect the annual tribute for the governor. When Peralta complained, Ordóñez excommunicated him.

Not long afterward, ignoring his excommunication, Peralta arrived at the church in Santa Fe for Mass and found that Ordóñez had arranged to throw the governor's chair out into the plaza. Peralta ordered his men to put it back in the church but in the rear among the Indians. The following day another quarrel erupted between the two men and Ordóñez publicly called Peralta a Lutheran, a heretic, and a Jew. In response, Peralta ordered Ordóñez out of town.

There followed some pushing and shoving, and Peralta's firearm discharged, wounding a soldier and a lay brother. Ordóñez excommunicated Peralta again (!) and locked the church down.

Peralta judged that the colony's existence (not to mention his own) was threatened by all this and decided to plead his case to the Viceroy in New Spain. But Ordóñez heard about his plan. Near Isleta, he and a gang of partisans captured Peralta and jailed him in Santo Domingo, where he languished for nine months. During this period, Ordóñez assumed command of the provincial affairs, both secular and religious—no doubt what he had intended for the Franciscan mission from the outset.

*Rock art of clown. Frijoles Canyon, rebellion era.*

A number of friars complained about Ordóñez's rough tactics, one of them suggesting that the letter Ordóñez had brought making him head of the religious affairs of the province was a forgery. While this all sounds ridiculous in retrospect—like the squabbles of kids in the schoolyard—the issue was an important one: who was first among governing entities, the civilian government or the friars?

In November 1614, Peralta escaped and reached Mexico City where, by 1617, he was exonerated by the court. That same year, Ordóñez was ordered back to Mexico City where he was reprimanded and banished from New Mexico. This pathetic affair helped launch a pattern of secular-ecclesiastic battles that would plague the colony for another sixty years. And, of course, it was under this oft-appearing cloud that the Franciscans had to undertake what they thought was their challenging and often very dangerous work of saving souls.

## *The Conversion Process*

At least one of the procedures Franciscans used for converting the natives of New Spain was not needed in New Mexico: reducing them, meaning moving them into towns. The friars could simply move into a pueblo and begin the process of establishing themselves as generous and powerful, even fascinating figures.

They would arrive bearing gifts—bells, beads, clothing of various kinds, scissors—knowing that the Pueblos and other Natives they had experience with took the idea of reciprocity very seriously. So from the start, the Pueblos were, in a small way at least, in the padres' debt. The Franciscans also brought—even as far back as Oñate—chili peppers and wheat, and later peach, plum, apricot, and cherry trees, along with vegetables like peas, cabbage, onions, garlic, radishes, and cucumbers. The friars also could "dazzle" (to use historian David Weber's apt word) the Pueblos with their bright ritual vestments along with elaborate ceremonies, paintings of religious figures, and music. Most of them were good performers and, with the help of a few soldiers or lay brothers, could put on mini-pageants that illustrated biblical tales. The Pueblos liked elaborate shows, either secular or religious, being experts at performances themselves.

Before long, some of the Pueblos would be persuaded to build a convent—that is, living quarters—for the friars, and then a church. In contradistinction from the kivas, which among the eastern pueblos were round, the churches were rectangular buildings made of adobe. Women did the brickwork in such buildings just as they did in the construction of their own homes. Men were trained in carpentry and other crafts. Soon, there were herds of sheep and cattle that needed tending, and the Pueblos learned a good deal about animal husbandry, with the supply of meat replacing the need to hunt. It is not surprising that many of the Pueblos would find the new foods, crafts, skills, and ceremonies pleasing. Imagine your first bite of a ripe peach after a lifetime of corn, beans, and squash. And the friars themselves would have seemed highly charismatic.

One tactic of the friars was to ingratiate themselves as best they could with the leaders of the pueblos, with the goal of eventually outdoing them in various ways and replacing them. Another ripe target was the children of the pueblos, innocent and therefore open minds that could most easily be persuaded by the pomp and fun and the promise of churchly events. They were taught to sit in class and learn Spanish and the catechism (at least by rote), and to sing hymns and even play some of the musical instruments the friars had brought with them. Once converted, the children might even (as they grew older) ridicule the old people and their traditional ways.

The friars explained, in Spanish and at least to adults and older children, that they could achieve immortality by putting their faith in Jesus Christ and the Church (meaning the friars in this case). Otherwise they would go to Hell, a place of fire and desperation, a place to which they would go even if they were baptized into the Holy Faith and then sinned and died unrepentant. No one really knows what the Pueblos made of this draconian geography. It is likely it struck them as bizarre because, in their view, everyone made a relatively smooth transition from living on earth in a bodily form to being a spirit. There were plenty of sinful things going on, the friars pointed out, that would keep the Pueblos out of heaven. For example, they complained about nakedness as well as what struck the friars as adultery and other sexual deviancies.

All of this and more, the friars believed, found full expression in the dances of the katsinas and other barbarous rites. Most if not all the Pueblos were polygamous at the time, and there was nakedness. How much is not truly known, and historians disagree. Some Spanish reports talk of girls going about naked until they were married. Other reports talk of women wearing apron-like skirts, but otherwise being unclad. In addition to all this, there are reports that sex was relatively free, women being convinced that bestowing sexual favors on men could calm down difficult moments, even enemies. Sexual intercourse, in this view, was the road to harmony. Modern-day Pueblos object to these characterizations as Spanish exaggerations or outright lies to make the Indians seem barbarous. Certainly the few Spanish descriptions of katsina dances ending in plaza-wide orgies of sex and incest are surely astounding exaggerations—or quite possibly mistakes in interpreting what were the antics of the clowns acting out increasing corruption.

In any event, the Franciscans not only wanted to replace the idolatrous religious practices of the Pueblos, which were clearly the work of the omnipresent Devil, but also all aspects of their non-European, barbarian way of life. The Indians needed to learn to wear proper clothes and shoes, to be modest, and to never engage in adultery. And how could there not be adultery in Spanish eyes if men could have several wives—a practice the padres called "concubinage." Instead, men were told they could have only one wife and that the union had to be sanctified by a Catholic wedding ceremony. This stricture would prove one of the most objectionable.

How did the Franciscans persuade the Pueblos to go along with these new prescriptions? How did they persuade them to stop their own labors and build churches to an unfamiliar god? To give up their several wives for one? To allow the friars to impose restrictions on their sex lives?

In many cases, they didn't. Some Pueblos were fully resistant from the start. The farther the pueblo from San Gabriel and then Santa Fe, and the later the friars arrived, the greater the resistance to their message. Taos in the north, Jemez in the northwest, and Zuni west of the Rio Grande were the most hostile to the Spanish. In some pueblos like Pecos, some individuals resisted while other members of the pueblo did not. Sometimes those who were averse to the new teachings left their home pueblos and took up residence at others.

Baptisms, catechism lessons, and church attendance on Sundays took place in many of the pueblos. Some of the converts, no doubt, were thoroughly persuaded and some may have actually rejected traditional ways. Others may have simply, open-mindedly, accepted both religious practices as not mutually exclusive. (Many Native Americans of the Southwest today profess traditional practices along with at least a lukewarm acceptance of Christianity or Mormonism or peyotism—known as the Native American Church—or all three. For many Indians, religion is a lot of fun, so the more the merrier. It is useful to remember that the katsina dances and other forms of what we call worship were also a preferred form of entertainment for Pueblo spectators.)

Most likely, the Pueblos knew how difficult the soldiers and the friars could make life for them if they didn't at least pretend to go along—to pay lip service as well as labor to the friars and their new religion. Memories are long in such places, and the stories of Oñate's retaliation for one "sin" or another at Acoma and among the Tompiro pueblos, not to mention Coronado's devastation of the Tiguez pueblos fifty years earlier, were horror tales known by all.

The friars also emerged as men with considerable supernatural powers. Diseases like smallpox occasionally erupted and devastated the Pueblos but not—notably—the Franciscans. Where the Franciscans came from, smallpox had essentially become a children's disease of diminished power, rendering them mostly immune, making them appear to have very special powers in the eyes of the Pueblos. Even the Franciscans' devotion to chastity called for superhuman willpower. Most likely, the Pueblos gave up sex (and probably salt and meat) for a few days before an important ceremony or hunt, but total abstinence was probably unthinkable.

Though the Franciscans doled out some attractive carrots, they also resorted to the stick.

One of the most powerful sticks the friars wielded was, in fact, a pair of shears. Most Pueblos wore their hair long with bangs, in some cases in braids or trimmed off around the jaw line. While few of the Franciscans ever bothered to learn the language of their flock, they were typically astute enough to learn a few Pueblo customs and mind-sets that they could make use of. To make a lasting impression by means of humiliation, the friars would have a transgressor's hair shorn, a punishment that most Pueblos probably looked on as worse than a mere flogging and in some instances worse than death.

All such punishment was universally seen by the Pueblos as an affront to their dignity, as were the draconian rules of unbreakable marriages to only one wife. However, even more debasing were those times when the friars marched into pueblo homes and storerooms, rounded up the Pueblos' sacred and healing objects, and made bonfires of them in the village plaza. After decades of Spanish missionizing, one European wrote that most of the Pueblo people "have never forsaken idolatry, and they appear to be Christians more by force than to be Indians who are reduced to the Holy Faith."

Even so, the colony of New Mexico took on a rejuvenated if wobbly course after the Peralta-Ordóñez period. It was accompanied by what might well have been called the golden age of mission building. One of the most glorious examples of mission building (though it got off to a shaky start) took place in the relatively sophisticated pueblo that lay on the eastern edge of pueblo country on a small rocky mesa lying between two high, evergreen-covered escarpments, a sentinel looking eastward to the buffalo plains: Pecos.

## *The Golden Age of Mission Building*

In a 1622 letter to the Viceroy in Mexico, the Franciscan who had been assigned to Galisteo pueblo complained that the current governor of New Mexico, Peralta's replacement, was "a bag of arrogance and vanity without love for God."[8] The governor in question was Don Juan de Eulate, and the angry friar was Fray Pedro Zambrano Ortiz. Zambrano spoke for most of the friars who were convinced that Eulate was a blasphemous monster who encouraged the natives to perform their dances and other devilish rites for no other reason than to weaken the influence of the Franciscans. At the same time, Governor Eulate encouraged forced labor, even the kidnapping of Pueblo children for that purpose, and cared not at all for such matters as Native rights that were mandated by the Crown. He was, in short, a thug.

Zambrano was assigned to Pecos pueblo in 1617. His first task at Pecos was to build a convent, as preparation to building a mission church. Rather than move into the pueblo itself—it is not clear whether this was his choice or that of the Pueblo inhabitants—he built these modest living quarters at the south end of the pueblo on an old ruin. That Zambrano had any success in his missionary duties is remarkable, given the pervasive sabotage of such efforts by Governor Eulate, whom a twentieth-century scholar, France V. Scholes, described as a "petulant, tactless, irreverent soldier whose actions were inspired by open contempt for the Church and its ministers."[9]

In 1620, Zambrano was transferred to nearby Galisteo. He traded places with an enthusiastic and youthful friar, the 27-year-old Fray Pedro de Ortega. Fray Pedro had had a bad year at Galisteo, unable to stem the Indians' pagan religion. He was determined not to give in at Pecos. In 1621, Pecos was still one of the largest of all the pueblos, with some two thousand souls.

Appearing twenty-odd years after the arrival of the Spanish, young Fray Pedro represented the first significant attempt to establish the Church in the midst of the Pecos people, many of whom were traders and therefore a bit more worldly than most Pueblo people. As the easternmost pueblo, Pecos was a major trading site with the Apaches who would arrive annually from the plains, usually in late August or September, laden with buffalo hides, jerked meat, and tallow (solid fat of cattle for soap or candles) to trade for pueblo corn, squash, and beans. By this time, the Spanish colonists as well as the Pueblo people used animal hides of all sorts for clothing and other purposes.

In any event, they were maintaining their traditional ceremonies when Fray Pedro moved into the convent south of town, and he launched a frontal attack on the pueblos' rampant idolatry and paganism, seizing idols, effigies, masks, and other ceremonial paraphernalia. Why the throngs at Pecos allowed this to take place is anybody's guess. The pueblo may have been torn by factional strife—some deep-seated issue unknown to any Spanish chronicler—and was thus unable to complain or act as a single community. Like small towns everywhere, pueblos often split into factions over one issue or another, usually doctrinal.

Despite the difficulties, Fray Pedro went on to lay out a great church, choosing the site not far south of the pueblo proper and staking out the foundations. It was to be big enough to seat all two thousand members of the pueblo, a major example of priestly ambition on two counts: it would be the biggest such building in the province, and soon, he dreamed, it would fill with happy and worshipful Pecos Christians.

Before Fray Pedro could do more, for reasons that are unclear, the custodia assigned him to Taos pueblo in the north, where he was greeted by intransigent tribal members who refused him lodging, fed him tortillas made with urine and mouse meat, and demanded that he leave. Suffering these indignities, including a near miss in an assassination attempt, all of which he wrote about to his superiors in New Spain, the youthful Franciscan persevered and, most likely through acts of priestly kindness, eventually won over some of the Taos people for a while.

Meanwhile the new friar at Pecos was Fray Andrés Juárez, an older hand who had survived a number of run-ins (including a jail term) with governor Eulate's predecessor, the dreaded Ordóñez. When Fray Andrés took over at Pecos, he took no destructive actions against idolatry but instead decided to learn the language of the Pecos people and let the grace of God lead them to salvation.

Fray Andrés begged his superiors all the way up to the Viceroy in New Spain for the resources to build what would become the most monumental building in all of North America. In writing to the Viceroy, he said the church's altarpiece should be installed in the Viceroy's name, pointing out that every year hordes of Apache heathens came to trade, bringing skins and other things of value to the pueblos and the Spaniards. The Apaches, Fray Andrés wrote, would enter the church where "the Lord will enlighten them so that they want to be baptized and converted to Our Holy Catholic Faith,"[10] a most desirable outcome thanks to the altarpiece installed in the Viceroy's name. Egos being what they are, materials and funds began to flow north, and the gigantic church began to rise from the bedrock.

The church would be forty-one feet across at the east-facing entrance to the nave, tapering to thirty-seven feet across at the sanctuary. To accommodate Pecos' population, the church would be an astounding 145 feet long. At forty feet or so in height, it would be visible for miles, the high ceiling bespeaking God's glory in an extravagant volume of empty space, previously unimaginable to the Pueblo people with their low-ceilinged, almost claustrophobic rooms. To accomplish such height, the walls needed to be especially thick—eight feet wide at the top and, to support the towers that would rise above the roof, twenty-two feet wide at the ground level. In all, this meant over three hundred thousand adobe bricks were needed, each weighing about forty pounds. Crenellated at the top with buttresses along the side walls, the church would more closely resemble a fortress than any church in Europe. When finished it was one of the largest—and almost surely the single most imposing—building up to that time on the North American continent.

The builders of these astonishingly high walls were women. Men hauled earth and water to make the adobe bricks, and wood to build the needed scaffolding, as well as long straight tree trunks to be laid across the walls to hold up the roof. The Pecos cadre of skilled carpenters would go on to help erect many mission churches and buildings in other pueblos.

Construction was completed in 1625, having been slowed by periodic harassment by Governor Eulate who verbally and often physically threatened those engaged in the building or those who offered the use of their oxen to help. Eulate complained that building such grandiose churches—similar work was by now under way in several other pueblos—using the free labor of the Pueblos, denied them the necessary time to work their fields. However accurate Eulate's complaints were, they were surely offered not out of concern for the Indians but simply out of Eulate's overweening anticlericalism.

The final "magnificent temple" was described with superlatives by all Europeans who saw it. Historian Kessell wrote that the Pecos church "became at once a revelation and a focus," bespeaking "plainly a virile God who had shown His followers many advanced ways . . . the towering new church epitomized the strong ministry of Andrés Juárez,[11] who would serve the people of Pecos for thirteen years, a relatively long term for a Franciscan to remain in one place. After the church was completed, along with a more elaborate series of church-related buildings, the Christianized members of Pecos began to build homes in its vicinity at the south end of the pueblo.

A later witness to the Franciscans' mission-building program described the daily peopling of these Christian communities in action:

More than twenty Indians, devoted to the service of the church, live with [the friar] in the *convento*. They take turns relieving one another as porters, sacristans, cooks, bell-ringers, gardeners, waiters, and at other tasks. They perform their duties with much attention and care as if they were friars ... In every pueblo where a friar resides, he has schools for the teaching of prayer, choir, playing musical instruments, and other useful things ... All go into the church, and the friar says Mass and administers the sacraments ... At mealtime, the poor people in the pueblo who are not ill come to the porter's lodge, where the cooks of the convento have readied sufficient food, which is served to them by the friar ...[12]

Even with the imposing architectural, administrative, and ministerial presence in the grand mission church at Pecos, however, not all the Pecos people went along with the Franciscan scheme of things. Two factions seem to have existed even before the arrival of Spaniards and persisted under Spanish control. The traders were more worldly and liberal, traveling to the far reaches of the familiar world, and to these were suddenly added the skilled guild of carpenters, called on to work in many other pueblos. For such traveled folk, the bonds of agriculture—and the communitarian principles of Pueblo life and psychology developed to sustain it—were necessarily loosened.

Even so, the decade of the 1620s was a golden age of church building in New Mexico. The church bells, cast in bronze and hauled a thousand miles from New Spain, would toll at intervals throughout each day for another half-century or so, summoning the faithful for lessons, hymns, prayers, and colorful ritual. But so far as can be discovered, the tolling of the bells, audible for miles through the bone-dry air, failed to summon the hearts of most of the Pueblo people, even those raising their voices to sing praise up into the high reaches of the angelic white-plastered temples of the foreign God.

# CHAPTER 6

# *A Franciscan Pitchman*

FRAY ALONSO BENAVIDES, who arrived in New Mexico in 1626, would have loved to see New Mexico and the lands stretching east across the plains into what is now the Texas panhandle as one great ecclesiastic unit with him installed as its bishop.

A drawing of unknown accuracy shows Fray Alonso as a slender man with dark eyebrows, heavily lidded eyes, and thin lips. His hands are large, with the look of labor on them. Benavides was Portuguese, born in the Azores in 1578, and he turned up in New Spain in 1598, the same year Oñate took on the colonization of the remote province of Nueva Mexico. By 1603, Benavides was a member of the Franciscan order and worked in various provinces of New Spain for more than a decade and a half before being selected to take charge of New Mexico.

Fray Alonso was an optimist. The poverty of these arid and unpromising lands—and the recalcitrance of some of the Pueblo people to fully accept the teachings of the Church—were no deterrent to him. He was also, on behalf of this dream, an enthusiastic promoter, given to stretching certain facts, and a gifted fundraiser. Even before he actually reached New Mexico in 1626, he had already secured the wherewithal to bring twelve friars with him on the thousand-mile trek from Mexico to Santa Fe. In the artful traditions of the Church, the twelve friars symbolized the Twelve Apostles, making their arrival all the more significant.

So successful was Fray Alonso that after his tenure in New Mexico in 1629, he would persuade the cash-strapped Spanish Crown to finance another *thirty* Franciscan missionaries to expand on the order's already notable successes, which he described with appealing enthusiasm (and what appears now to have been a free-wheeling exaggeration). It was not miracles he exaggerated;

naturally enough, Fray Alonso believed implicitly in miracles. It was numbers—particularly the numbers of Indians who he claimed had been successfully baptized and saved from savagery and Satan.

Benavides arrived on foot in Santa Fe on January 26, 1626, greeted there with elaborate pomp and ceremony. He was the third custodian of missions for the province of New Mexico and also the first agent of the Inquisition in the province, the claim of Ordóñez having been a total fraud. Wherever a large presence of the Church arose in such a place as New Mexico, the Inquisition would soon be established. The function was not to put idolaters to death at the fiery stake nor to torture them by various means, including waterboarding them. In New Mexico, the Inquisition's role was to act as independent investigators of the religious and sectarian leaders and the colonists, to see that they operated lawfully. Later, New Mexican agents of the Inquisition would use the powers of this institution to flay the secular authorities in Santa Fe (typically overlooking any wrong-doing by individual Franciscans). But Benavides would devote his inquisitional efforts mostly to local cases of witchcraft and other unseemly minor crimes by the local Hispanic populace rather than use the Inquisition as a blunt political tool. As always, the wheels of justice turned exceedingly slow.

## The Strenuous Journey

The wagon trains, organized by the Franciscans, were supposed to arrive from New Spain every three years, but overcoming various common bureaucratic delays had taken Benavides two years to get this train organized. As pointed out by Baker Morrow, the latest translator of Benavides's Memorial of 1630 (a memorial being a cross between a report and a memoir), these year-long journeys were almost unimaginably arduous. Livestock needed to be fed and watered as the wagon train progressed a few miles each day. The wind and sun ruined clothes and human skin; subtropical animals and people had to adapt to increasingly intense cold, especially at night; and animals and people could drown in suddenly surging streams.

The journeys needed to be timed to reach El Paso del Norte before—or after—the Rio Grande reached its springtime high, when floodwaters made crossing it impossible. Everything except people and livestock was carried in large, heavy wagons with irregularly round wooden wheels that screeched in protest continuously, an awful sound that carried for miles. Newcomers were always surprised that the New Mexicans didn't mind the racket the wagons made, some calling them "singing" wagons. The mules pulling the wagons would add to the cacophony, while the air, lungs, and clothing filled with choking dust.

It is known today (from various experiments in group living such as Biosphere II and some NASA projects) that six or more people, if thrown together in close quarters for more than six months, erupt into factions based on irrational angry disputes. The journeys to New Mexico provided a severe test for even the most congenial, and as often as not the religious and secular members of the wagon train did not see eye to eye.

Fray Alonso Benavides evidently took these rigors in stride. He did, however, write of the wild tribes along the way who were given to attacking the wagon trains. Benavides typically sought, among these hostile groups, "the conversion of redeemable souls"[13] and with some success, he introduced them to the healing powers of the Cross and looked forward to the time when "His Divine Majesty can work His marvels in a place like that, confirming the promise of His Holy World."[14] All things, he was saying, in their time.

In any event, Benavides recognized that without the regular arrival of the wagon trains with food, tools, new colonists, and religious artifacts (like the brass bells to be installed in the growing number of mission churches) the effort to make New Mexico a religious as well as commercial success would falter if not fail altogether. In messages from New Mexico, and especially in the Memorial for the King of Spain that Benavides wrote in 1630, he complained of the laggardly supply trains and the lack of enough Franciscans to convert all the Native people in the region, not just the Pueblos. He also drew attention, as had most Franciscan custodians before him, to the need for more protection of the Pueblos from unnecessarily harsh treatment by the Spanish governors of the province.

## Fray Benavides and the Pueblo Miracles

Benavides was, it seems, a particularly kindly man. He saw the good in the lowliest Indian, had high praise for the friars who risked so much to bring souls to the Cross, and took delight in much of what he saw in New Mexico, including an attribute of the Natives that is virtually never discussed in any of the Spanish accounts: their sense of the ridiculous. In the Memorial from which most quotations of his words come, he wrote of an old sorcerer who approached him, looking angry, and said loudly:

"'You Spaniards and Christians are crazy; you desire and pretend that this pueblo should also be crazy.' I asked him in what respect we were crazy . . . he answered me: 'How are you crazy? You go through the streets in groups, flagellating yourselves, and it is not well that the people of this pueblo should commit such madness as spilling their own blood by scourging themselves.' When he saw that I laughed, as did those around me, he ran out of the pueblo, saying he did not wish to be crazy."[15]

All in all, as Benavides proceeded around the Rio Grande pueblos where the friars had concentrated most of their efforts before the 1620s, he was pleased as punch with what he saw. In pueblo after pueblo, he was delighted to hear the children singing canticles and happy to be cheerfully greeted by Indians with praise for God. It was, he wrote, as if the Indians had been Christians for a hundred years.

He focused his own missionary efforts on the southern Piro-speaking pueblos, which were mostly without missions in their midst—a surprising lack, historians have noted, since these were the first pueblos seen by anyone arriving in the region. Possibly, they had been seen as too small to justify building a mission. Also, he pushed the building of missions among the Tompiro pueblos, the ones lying south of today's Albuquerque and east of the river and what are today called the Manzano Mountains.

To the King, he sang the praises of the seraphic order (meaning the angelic order of Franciscans) for their efforts. In thirty years, and "in only one district of a hundred leagues, our order has baptized more than eighty thousand souls and built more than fifty churches, all with excellent friaries. We have pacified more than five hundred thousand Indians."[16]

These last were the Apaches who lived in the hinterlands around the pueblo areas, and some hunting and gathering tribes in the south and east called "Jumanos." Benavides had taken a great interest in these people, describing several successful conversions of Apaches and Jumanos and calling for many more friars, the better to see that all of these tribes were converted. Of course there were nowhere near five hundred thousand Apaches and other regional tribes. The Apaches lived in relatively small bands, consisting of an extended family, and each band patrolled a large area. There were probably no more than five thousand of them at any time during the Spanish occupation of New Mexico—if that many.

Benavides described his wonder when a number of Jumanos approached him and asked for friars to come and baptize them properly. They knew a great deal already about the Cross and various other Christian matters. Asked how they knew this, they reported that a woman in blue had frequently visited them over the years, telling them about the ceremonies and beliefs of the Church. This was the legendary "Blue Lady," a Poor Clare nun who began visiting the southern tribes of New Mexico by divine transport beginning in about 1620, speaking of Christ and other churchly matters in their language.

Once he was back in Spain in 1629, Benavides would visit a Poor Clare abbess, Mother María de Ágreda, and satisfy himself that she was in fact the Blue Lady and had an excellent recall of many details of landscape and people of the area she had visited between 1620 and 1623. In a later expanded version of his Memorial, Benavides told the King of this remarkable, miraculous woman. The legend of the Blue Lady has persisted until modern times in the American Southwest even though, later in life, Mother María herself published a document denying that she had ever had such experiences.

In any event, as a man of the late Middle Ages and not of the Renaissance underway in Europe, Benavides wrote matter-of-factly of several miracles that had aided the friars' efforts at converting the Indians. In one of these, which took place in the Hopi village of Awatovi, the Franciscan was called a liar by the Hopi sorcerers who challenged him to heal the sight of a boy who had been born blind, his eyes never opening. If the friar failed to cure the boy's blindness, he would be killed. According to Benavides, "the padre fell on his knees with all the worry and devotion that you might imagine in a case like this." He beseeched the Divine Majesty for a miracle and placed his cross on the boy's eyes. "He opened them and began to cry aloud, admiring everything he saw."[17]

Everyone in the village then became Christian and called their sorcerers "lying deceivers." *Sit nomen Domini benedictum.* (Blessed be the name of the Lord.)

In another instance, at Taos Pueblo, the farthest pueblo from the Hopi mesas, way off to the east and north, several Christian women were returning to the pueblo in the company of a Taos woman who had not accepted baptism. She was talking about the joys of the old ways before the friars came and tried to change everything. Suddenly the Divine Majesty sent a lightning bolt that struck down the temptress, and the good Christian women, miraculously unharmed, were rendered all the stronger in their faith.

*Cross found in Apache country near Pecos*

Fray Alonso left the region in 1629, happy with the progress he saw and had in part impelled in New Mexico. He wrote his highly positive report to the King, even extolling the fertility of the region and the richness of the mines located in the mountains near the pueblo of Socorro (which in fact were not mineable. The refining process in those days called for the use of mercury, but mercury was not to be found in the ground in New Mexico, and it was carefully hoarded by mine owners in New Spain).

Benavides goes down in history as one of the greatest promoters of New Mexico of all time. This good-natured friar did finally get his bishopric but it was in Goa, a Portuguese holding on the Indian subcontinent. On his way there by ship, he disappeared from the face of the earth, no doubt lost in a shipwreck. But as he left New Mexico in 1629, thirty new friars arrived, primed to continue the golden age of mission building. Some of them had their eyes turned to the west where Acoma, the Zuni villages, and the distant Hopi villages waited, edgy places in difficult terrain, curious, proud, cloaked in ancient tradition, and given to long memories and suspicious dispositions— good places for martyrdom.

As it turned out, however, the next decades would hold a far more devastating fate for the Pueblo people than any martyrdom suffered by the Franciscans.

# CHAPTER 7

# *Completing the Cross*

ALL ACROSS THE LAND OF NEW MEXICO, from Taos to the Hopi villages, in the Spanish haciendas and mission churches, and in the poor and simple homes of the Hispanic colonists, the world was a place of omens, signs, and predictions. Perhaps the most implausible but powerful of all the signs in these times was a cartographic one, first noted by a Franciscan who is evidently unknown to history. He saw, lying across the province of New Mexico, a giant cross, delineated by the pueblos and, importantly, by the missions erected to lead the Indians into the arms of the Church.

The north–south axis of the cross extended from Taos south to Senecú. The east–west axis ran from the Tompiro pueblos east of the Río del Norte to the distant pueblos of the west—Acoma, Zuni, Hopi. Here then, almost miraculously, was a gigantic sign of God's intent, seen from a viewpoint beyond the eyes of men, indeed, God's view of the holy Franciscan enterprise in New Mexico.

With the departure of Fray Alonso Benavides, whose efforts had led to the building of Piro and Tompiro missions, the great cross lying across the land was three-quarters complete. And in 1629, as Benavides walked with the caravan returning to New Spain, a grand expedition began its long trek west to complete this cosmic imperative. It consisted of a small military escort, a handful of Franciscans including the Franciscan custodian, Estéban de Perea, and the new governor of New Mexico, Francisco Manuel de Silva Nieto. The grand procession was designed to impress the western Pueblo Indians, and its intent was to establish permanent Franciscan presence in these western pueblos.

It was not the first time the Spanish had made an effort to missionize these people. As early as 1599, a brother had been assigned by Oñate to minister to the western pueblos, but there is no record of his reaching any of them. By

1620, by which time some of the disfigured and indentured had filtered back to the great redoubt (stronghold) of Acoma and begun to rebuild the pueblo, another friar reported that he had visited there and was (not surprisingly) greeted with hostility. He claimed that he overcame the resistance and pacified the pueblo for a season, which sounds a bit like Franciscan spin.

In July of 1629, one of the new infusion of thirty friars from Mexico City evidently peeled off from the procession and made his way up the great rampart of Acoma. This was Fray Juan Ramírez, who might well have wondered what reception he would receive from the Acoma people, who, like most people brutalized by an occupying force, have long memories. But Fray Juan was fortunate enough to perform two miracles almost immediately. As he was reaching the top of the precipitous trail to the pueblo, a young Acoma woman accidentally dropped her baby over the edge, and the friar miraculously caught it. Once at the top, he met a young mother whose infant was sick and apparently dying in her arms. Ramírez persuaded her to let him baptize the child, which he did, and it promptly revived.

And so Fray Juan was welcomed into the pueblo that, up to this time, had had the greatest reason to be suspicious of the Spaniards and all their work. Under his direction, the people of Acoma built a church more than a hundred feet long, thirty-five feet high, with twin towers rising yet higher. The huge timbers for its roof were hauled from Mount Taylor thirty miles away, without (the story goes) their being allowed to touch the ground. Huge quantities of sand and water were hauled up the mesa to make the adobe bricks. At some points, the walls of the church were nine feet thick to support the great weight.

Fray Juan Ramírez remained at Acoma for about twenty years, helping with the rebuilding of the pueblo, and he imported herds of burros, sheep, and cows, along with fruit trees—pear, plum, peach, apricot, cherry, fig, and date. All of this was maintained below the mesas, as were the traditional fields of corn, beans, and melons, the old pueblo staples, now greatly improved in variety. Fray Juan was evidently much admired, though not all the residents were converted to the Church, a situation that existed in virtually all the pueblos. Reports from Acoma suggest that the pueblo included a significant group of "delinquents and apostates,"[18] and it is certain that Ramírez and those who followed him built up some animosity by discouraging the Acomas' traditional religious and marital practices. How deep those resentments ran would not be realized until later.

## *From Acoma to Zuni*

Looking west from the aerie-like vantage point of Acoma, the land stretches far off across a jumble of flat land and mesas, beyond which lies a shiny black badland where a volcano (Mount Taylor) once spread its ebony blood across the landscape. Fifty miles or so beyond the treacherous lava flow were the lands of the Zuni. People from Acoma made regular journeys to the land of the Zunis for trade and especially to a brine lake fifty miles south of Hawikuh where salt whitened the shores—what was then and remains today some of the purest sodium chloride in nature.

Hopis, Apaches, and others also trekked to this lake for the salt, along pathways worn into the earth and still in use today. The paths were a safe zone: no matter what hostility one bore for someone on any of the paths, there could be no violence. These paths are the Southwestern version of the *calumet* (peace pipe) of the northeast and plains, the smoking of which made conflict temporarily unthinkable.

In those days, Hawikuh was one of six Zuni pueblos all ranged along the perennially running Zuni River. Governor Oñate had been welcomed there on his first journey west, the Zunis no doubt wanting to avoid any more trouble from the prickly and vengeful Spaniards. Then, for three decades they, like the Hopis and Acomas, were left to their own devices. But with the effort in 1629 to complete the great pueblo cross, they received a visitation, and an impressive one.

At Zuni, the military escort, Governor Nieto, and other civilian officers proceeded in turn to kneel before the Franciscans and kiss their feet, "to make these people," the custodian Fray Estéban later wrote, "understand the true veneration that they should show the friars whenever they met them."[19]

The Spanish could soon satisfy themselves that their theatrical object lesson bore fruit because within less than three years the Zunis had erected a hundred-foot-long church with an additional six rooms. For a town of six or seven hundred people, this was a mighty labor. A mission was also built in nearby Halona—the present-day pueblo of Zuni. All this was a tribute to the perseverance of Fray Francisco Estrada and a fellow priest, Martín de Arvide. Yet whatever

*Stylized eagle feathers from Hawikuh pottery*

enthusiasm some of the Zunis brought to these tasks, others more than likely resented the Spanish presence from the outset and smoldered with hate. In February 1632, the people of Hawikuh (or at least a faction in the village) murdered both Franciscans, scalping and decapitating them, and cutting off their hands and feet.

Fearing indiscriminate reprisals, the Zunis all fled for a time to a high promontory in the area called "Dowa Yalanne" (referred to as Corn Mountain in English). But no replacements for the priests showed up, and no soldiers either. The Zunis would be left alone again until 1660 when missionaries returned. A pattern was emerging. The farther a pueblo or group of pueblos was from the main center of the Spanish occupation, the more resistant they were to real conversion and the more accomplished they tended to be as creators of Franciscan martyrdom.

In any event, in 1629, having established the missions in Zuni, the grand procession continued west to the Hopis, the most remote and in some ways most complicated of all the Pueblo people living under what passed for Spanish authority.

## Hopi Outposts

A hundred and twenty miles to the west and north of Zuni, the Hopi villages sat amid yellow sandstone mesas that preside over high desert scrubland and dry washes. In those days just about everyone called the people *Moquis*. The word had been pronounced Mo-kwee, but after a while it came to be pronounced Mo-kee, quite probably by the Spaniards. Not until late in the nineteenth century did people realize that the Hopis found the term offensive because, pronounced Mo-kee, it is very close to a Hopi word for "dead." But in those old days, they were called Moquis and the insult was the least of their problems.

In all, there were five Hopi villages when the Spanish arrived, linked loosely by language and tradition but each an independent unit, just as the Tewa-speaking pueblos of the Río del Norte were independent entities. Some of the Hopi villages had formed because of intravillage squabbles—usually over the proper way of being a Hopi. The westernmost of the villages at that time, Oraibi, was established when two brothers in an earlier village, Shungopavi, fell out, with one moving west to another mesa to start his own village. Over the years, other Native groups would show up at one or the other of the villages and, if they could show that they had something of value—typically a ceremony or some special knowledge—they would be taken in and become one of the thirty or so Hopi clans. Thus, the Hopi villages were populated.

In those days the people nearest the Hopis were the Zunis, about 120 miles to their southeast (a two-day run), and the Havasupais, a non-pueblo tribe who lived the same distance to the Hopis' west in a beautiful side canyon of Grand Canyon. It was a place of great lushness thanks to a fast-moving river that bursts downward in several spectacular waterfalls before flowing into the Colorado River.

The Hopis' relative isolation suited them for many reasons, chief among them being that they were far from people like Utes and Apaches who meant them harm. The price of seclusion was that they lived in the driest and most parsimonious landscape of all the pueblo-dwelling people. Neither rivers nor perennial streams ran through their part of the world; no water stood long in puddles. A few channels carried off a bit of spring run-off, but they were bone dry most of the year. The Hopis dry-farmed, planting seeds far apart in the sand of dry washes and counting on two or three timely sprinkles of rain in spring and summer to grow an astonishing quantity of corn, beans, and squash in sandy spots on the surrounding desert. The few springs near the villages produced some water, but it was too precious for irrigation.

To succeed as farmers in such a place took a lot of engineering, most of it ceremonial in nature. It is unlikely that any of the other Pueblo people— even the Zunis—enjoyed so elaborate a katsina presence as the Hopis did. The katsinas who materialized and danced in the Hopi villages also appeared in the sky as clouds, and the katsinas' songs were often about moisture, along with reminding the people of the proper Hopi way to live. Such preoccupations are unlikely to change much over time, so long as agriculture is both a central activity and a successful one.

## Spaniards on the Hopi Mesas

The Hopis' first taste of the Spanish had come when Coronado sent a lieutenant, Pedro de Tovar, and twenty-one soldiers from Zuni to inspect what the Zunis claimed were seven villages to the north and what Coronado was led to hope were the very seven cities of gold that the Zuni villages had turned out not to be. Tovar arrived below the easternmost village of Awatovi, situated on a high mesa. The Hopis came down, and there was bloodshed before things settled down to a bit of mutual gift giving, during which Tovar learned of a "big river" to the north, which he assumed was the much-sought-after opening to the South Sea.

Another Coronado lieutenant named Cárdenas was later dispatched to Awatovi where the friendly Hopis led him to the Grand Canyon, which the Spaniards viewed from above. A story goes that Cárdenas sent some men down to get water from the little stream they perceived at the canyon's bottom and they returned only after several days, having struggled a mile down into the Grand Canyon and back up. The Spanish, the story says, had nothing in their experience to let them perceive the vast scale of the canyon, which is a mile deep.

In fact, the Spanish could not find a trail down into the canyon and the Hopi guides gave them no help in this, though they were perfectly familiar with the canyon from making regular pilgrimages into it for salt and other purposes.

Other Spaniards came and went: a man named Espejo, who took possession of Hopi for the King and the Pope in 1583, and then vanished, and Oñate, who sojourned there briefly in 1599 on his way west seeking mining country.

## Missionaries to the Hopis

It was not until 1629, almost a century after the first Spaniards turned up on the Hopis' eastern flank, that the Spanish came to Hopiland with the intention of staying for good. Three religious (as they were sometimes called, the adjective used as a noun) arrived accompanied by twelve soldiers, and they were not gladly welcomed. One was a lay brother; the others were Fray Francisco Porras and Fray Andreas Guitérrez. Fray Porras was evidently a man of great intelligence, character, and dedication, but he had been preceded at Hopi by an apostate Indian from the east, a man who one chronicler of the time called "a tool of the devil." This man, whose name and tribe is lost to history, warned the Hopis that the soon-to-arrive Spaniards would burn their pueblos, steal their property, and behead their children. The friars, the warning continued, would attempt to sprinkle the Hopis' heads with some special water that would surely kill them.

The Hopis almost surely recalled that not so long ago two of their villagers had returned from Acoma and the Spanish court in Santo Domingo without their right hands. The Hopis would be all the more susceptible to believing the dire words of the apostate Native American messenger. Hostility simmered as the friars and the soldiers simply moved into Awatovi. The Spanish had to post guards night and day. But then the miracle that Fray Alonso Benavides described took place—the story of the blind boy being rendered able to see. The Hopis at Awatovi are said to have rejoiced and henceforth accepted whatever the Franciscans instructed.

First off, a mission church had to be built. Since the Franciscans had arrived on the feast day of San Bernardo of Clairvaux, the church would be dedicated to him. The extent to which the friars convinced the people of Awatovi of the value of the new faith over the old is to be seen in the placement of the mission. A central kiva—rectangular and with elaborate murals of katsinas and other figures—dominated the village and, at Fray Porras's request, the villagers filled the entire kiva with sand. Fray Porras then located the main altar of the new church directly above the buried kiva.

Whether the miracle with the blind boy ever occurred or not, the story was believed, and Fray Porras's deep devotion and outstanding probity among his peers were said to have brought the village of Awatovi firmly into the fold. Eventually, one of eighteen two-hundred-pound bells hauled from Mexico City to New Mexico in 1627 was installed in the church of San Bernardo de Aguatubi (aka Awatovi) which grew into an impressive structure with two bell towers, a side altar, quarters for the Franciscans, other quarters for the soldiers, pens for sheep, and various workrooms.

Soon, given the flowering of faith in Awatovi, the Franciscans prevailed on the Hopis to build missions in two of the other villages, including Oraibi, and *visitas* (smaller churches without full-time friars in residence) in the other two villages. But the other four villages never developed the zeal of the Awatovis; they remained suspicious of the entire Christian enterprise. Indeed, Fray Alonso Benavides, in his updated Memorial to the King, wrote that Hopi sorcerers managed to martyr Fray Porras by poisoning him in June 1633, only four years after he arrived. It remains possible that he died of natural causes.

Suspicious and hostile or not, all the Hopis benefited from the Franciscan presence, receiving metal tools such as knives, axes, chisels, and picks for woodworking and stoneworking. In addition, they received domestic animals— sheep and cattle—as well as new plant foods such as peaches. But with the benevolent Fray Porras gone, other friars were sent to continue the conversion of the Hopis and friction grew, occasionally breaking out into violence—or silliness.

In one instance at Awatovi, a Hopi called Juan, in the spirit of the clowns who irritate and taunt the katsinas, took over the congregation one day when the padre was elsewhere. He donned vestments, waived the incense burner, said the *Salve*, and sprinkled holy water all around. No doubt the assembled Hopis, though devout, thought this act wonderfully funny. But Juan was caught in this blasphemy by the resident friar, accused as well of sexual impropriety, and shipped off to Santa Fe for some heavy-duty behavioral rehabilitation at a convent there.

Whatever Juan's transgressions really were, they were nothing like what might be called "the Sixto affair," involving Fray Alonso de Posadas, who spent two years as the resident friar at Awatovi beginning in 1653. It was said that he feared that a Hopi village leader named Sixto was "making trouble with" a Hopi woman called Isabel who was evidently Fray Alonso's mistress. The friar talked two of the officers of the guard into killing Sixto and then, fearing that they might spill the beans, he talked the mestizo who had been appointed alcalde mayor of the village into trying them on trumped up charges of disobedience. This was accomplished in summary fashion, and the two soldiers were promptly hanged. The Franciscan was soon accused of capital crimes, but nothing much came of it.

The act of cruelty that appears to have stuck in the Hopi memory most profoundly occurred in the 1650s in Oraibi where the friar, Fray Salvado de Guerra, presided. He evidently came upon an Oraibi man, Juan Cuna, involved in an act that he considered extremely idolatrous. One historian, Harry James, speculates that Cuna may have been carving a katsina doll.[*] In any event, Fray Salvado gave Cuna a public beating so severe that he was "bathed in blood," and then hauled him into the church and beat him once more. Then, to make sure everyone understood the seriousness of the offense, the friar doused Cuna with turpentine and set him on fire.

These brutal acts and others of a similar nature came to the attention of the Inquisition and Fray Salvado was removed from Awatovi and, as a punishment for murder, given a clerical assignment at the comfortable Franciscan (and Inquisition) headquarters in the pueblo of Santo Domingo, which lay alongside the cheerful, refreshing waters of the Río Bravo del Norte. Meanwhile, locals took measures to avoid religious conflicts.

---

[*] Hopi katsina dolls were always just toys, to be played with but of no sacred significance. It is only recently that commercial Hopi carvers have craftily allowed that there is some religious significance to them, and Hopi children now don't play with them but hang them on the walls of their houses.

## Secret Ceremonies

At the Hopi villages, as elsewhere in the pueblos to the east, the friars did their best to stamp out the pagan rites wherever they still occurred, burning ceremonial paraphernalia and, in many cases, Indians who used them in secret. As the years went by after the golden age of mission building, more and more friars had to deal with surreptitious reversions to the "idolatrous and devilish religious ceremonies" of their wards. The Hopis, rather than risk other acts of brutality, simply took their ceremonies elsewhere—to a place called Katsina Bluffs, several miles out on the painted desert to the west.

Katsina Bluffs is a large formation of red sandstone that seems to leap out of the desert. It looks like a solid red mesa. But once one is on top, it clearly is no standard tableland. Instead it consists of many narrow and curving paths of rock, some less than a yard across, that wind around like ribbon candy on its side, leaving dark little nooks and crannies straight down about three hundred vertiginous feet below. It is so dizzying a place seen from the top, so precipitous and convoluted, that it seems impossible that it could have been created by mere erosion.

Forbidden by the Franciscans from performing their sacred katsina dances, the Hopis took to trekking out to this bizarre landform and, hidden away in its folds, kept their traditions alive and vibrant, and kept the timely rains coming as best they could. There and at home on the mesas, the clan leaders and religious society leaders—men who had gone through life-threatening initiations to achieve their stations in Hopi society—would have swallowed their bile and bided their time.

Elsewhere, some of the Pueblo people were more impatient and the rifts that had always existed to some degree or other between the Pueblos and the Spanish began to tear open. As noted earlier, by 1632, Zunis at Hawikuh had martyred Fray Estrada and, having done so, enjoyed a long period without any interference from the Spanish. Much later, when another friar showed up at Zuni, he was dispatched to heaven by some Apaches. Indeed, Zuni vied with far-off and ever-recalcitrant Taos as among the most resistant to conversion and the most accomplished in creating martyrs. In 1639, people at Taos killed two priests and burned down the church. Rather than experience reprisals by the Spanish, they decamped to western Kansas where they stayed in an Apache settlement called El Cuartelejo for more than two decades. Jemez, those northwestern mountain folk who were also at an extreme edge of the Pueblo world, erupted in both 1644 and 1647, and a number of Tewa villages rose up in 1650.

## Growth and Change

In most parts of the Pueblo world of the 1630s and 1640s, society was changing rapidly and growing far more complicated. The Spanish governors appointed their own officers to Spanish-inspired offices for the governance of the pueblos, but these offices were added to the traditional and usually theocratic governments of the Indians, rather than replacing them. Pueblo warriors were expected to fight alongside the Spanish soldiers when it came to repelling attacks by the surrounding Apaches or, less frequently, the Utes from farther north. All of this provided the Pueblo Indians with experience of and insight into the Spanish ways of governing and waging war.

The so-called wild tribes, particularly the Apaches, also felt free to raid the pueblos from time to time, carrying off women and children whom they enslaved. The Spanish typically retaliated, carrying off women and children whom they enslaved, as well as shipping many south into New Spain where they disappeared into slavery, either in Spanish households or, in the case of men, into the bowels of the earth as miners of the silver so needed by the Spanish Crown. (Who started the slaving raids—Apaches, Spaniards, even Pueblos—is lost in the contentious murk of Southwestern history.)

Some of the slaves in Spanish households, particularly those who were from the plains originally, eventually spoke Spanish and acted like Spaniards. When they were given their freedom as adults, they found themselves socially neither Indian nor Spanish but in a kind of limbo, unwelcome in the pueblos and in Hispanic homes as well. They were called *Genízaros* and many were given land to build towns on—towns conveniently located between the Spanish settlements and the lands of the raiding wild tribes—cannon fodder, in other words.

The changing ethnicity of the Pueblo world was anything but simple. In the beginning, most of the colonists had been men so there was considerable intermarriage—soldiers and colonists intermarrying with mestiza women (Spanish and Mexican Indian) or with Pueblo women (creating Hispanics), or with blacks and mulattos, with varying quantities of blackness, or Indianness, or what have you, each kind with a slightly different station in life, and a different moniker. Hispanics, in particular, came to be highly numerous, taking important positions in the governance of the province, and some of them living comfortably in both worlds—the Spanish and the Pueblo.

Meanwhile, the Spanish *encomenderos* and the Franciscans continued to exact a great deal of effort and booty from their wards in the building of churches and the daily chores involved in running so large an enterprise. Pay for such labor had not changed in fifty years, plus the labor became all the more onerous as the years went by and the Native population was collapsing in numbers. Some sixty thousand people had inhabited the pueblos of 1600 and the numbers had not fallen significantly until the thirties and forties. But by mid-century the population (as counted in the confusing and complex ethnic combinations to be found in the pueblos) had dropped to some thirty thousand. Evidently there had been a terrible and relatively quick loss of Pueblo people, almost certainly the result of particularly virulent outbreaks of European diseases among the Pueblos, smallpox certainly and one attributed to anthrax.

People living in the close quarters of pueblos were perfect targets for the rapid spread of disease. Records are few and far between of the specific outbreaks. As historian Barbara Tuchman has pointed out in connection to the Black Plague of Europe, after such appalling events, the survivors tend to be speechless—literally. No one seems to talk about the horrors of it all.

In comparison to the psychological devastation of such sudden, inexplicable, and widespread death, other effects of population loss were more mundane but nevertheless of considerable importance. For example, while there were fewer people to work for the *encomenderos*, the demands were not reduced but increased, leaving fewer Pueblo workers with even less time to tend to their own fields. As a result they harvested less food, which put yet another strain on already stressed people. Disease and famine could have led many Pueblos to doubt that the Spanish, and in particular the friars, had enough power to help. Perhaps the new deities—Jesus and Mary—weren't all they had been cracked up to be. The ceremonial village leaders and the traditional ceremonies, even possibly the katsinas themselves, might not be up to keeping the world safe and productive anymore.

The precipitous decline in population also brought about the abandonment of numerous pueblos, especially in the east and south, with people streaming across the landscape looking for other less affected Pueblo people to move in with. Such refugees, uprooted and not especially welcome elsewhere, were typically viewed as second-class citizens, creating social tensions and adding to the general societal confusion. Losing half of the population in a matter of years called every feature of Pueblo life and every belief, old and new, into question. Some scholars of the period, and especially the demographer Elinore M. Barrett, believe this loss of population was the main catastrophe in the sad history of the Spanish province of New Mexico, that most unloved of colonies.

The pueblo world was, then, as the 1640s and 1650s moved toward the 1660s, simmering. Much of life was clearly out of anyone's control. A natural calamity such as prolonged drought, or a social or political event such as government bankruptcy, or an intensification of Apache raiding—any of these added to the travails of New Mexican life would be enough to bring that straitened, overworked, and fragile world to a lethal boil.

# CHAPTER 8

# The Promise and Failure of Don Bernardo

IF ANYONE HAD BEEN PLACED in time and geography to relieve the tensions building up in the polyglot pressure cooker of New Mexico in mid-century, it was Bernardo López de Mendizábal, the nineteenth governor of this province. Eighteen governors had come and gone, few of them rising to most occasions, and few of them distinguishing themselves as administrators, military officers, or even as especially clever thieves. They were not, typically, among New Spain's most accomplished, learned, or effective. Being governor of New Mexico was not the kind of job that set one on the career fast track.

Don Bernardo had the makings of what we might today call a celebrity–politician—wit, charisma, and a habit of speaking his mind bluntly on controversial matters. He was one of the most educated men ever to serve as New Mexico's colonial governor, and he had a well-honed sense of style as well as administrative experience.

Recall that the Renaissance, with its burgeoning reliance on reason, science, and the individual, was slow to arrive in the New World, and even slower to reach the remote province of New Mexico. Don Bernardo, in a sense, represented some of this new attitude and had a scorn for holdovers from the medieval times, particularly the kind of blind faith in revealed truths that characterized the world of monasteries and monks. His was an intellectual rejection of Catholic superstition, not a merely thuggish anti-clericalism like that of Eulate and others. Nevertheless, historians are generally agreed that Don Bernardo was a catastrophe. Historian John Kessell calls him "a petulant, strutting, ungracious *criollo* (a person of pure Spanish descent born in the Americas) with a sharp tongue and enough education to make himself dangerous."[20] But he did have—until the end—a lot of style. Had there been a press corps in New Mexico at the time, he would have been a media darling.

The newly appointed Governor López, then about forty years old, was transported northward from Mexico City starting on Christmas Eve of 1658 as part of the triennial supply caravan. As befitted his station, he traveled in a large covered wagon that stood out sharply among the caravan's rude wooden oxcarts, the few mounted soldiers, and the slow-moving livestock.

Riding with him, protected from some of the dust of the *Camino Real*, the Royal Road, was his wife, Doña Teresa Aguilera y Rocha. The two could luxuriate (comparatively speaking) in their comfortable bedding behind the wagon's curtains, attended at each stop by a *mulata* named Clarilla and a black woman named Ana de la Cruz. It was alleged later in complaints to the Inquisition in Santo Domingo that (however implausibly) the governor and his wife never once emerged from their wagon during the entire seven-month trip, not even to attend mass.

On June 30, 1659, the caravan reached Senecú, site of the southernmost Piro pueblo, now with its mission church, convent, and a handful of settlers. The people there welcomed the caravan with bells and horns, and the resident friar sprinkled the assemblage with holy water.

López was evidently unimpressed. He muttered that he would have expected a more elaborate welcome. Indeed, he may (as later reported) even have said he should be received "like the blessed Sacrament on the day of Corpus, with pallium and incense."[21] López wanted singing and dancing Indians, floral arches to pass beneath, the whole works—not just a modest clerical blessing outside the cemetery. People of the province who heard about this later were either scandalized by his sacrilege or amused by so bold a joke, depending on the intensity of their piety.

López carried on in his bratty way. That first night in Senecú, he was invited to a dinner put on by an eighty-year-old local widow and original settler, along with her daughter. He asked the two frontier ladies if they went to mass often. They replied that they attended as often as they could but sometimes failed to get there due to the lack of horses and mules. To this, López replied that they were healthier and better not going to mass, and should be happier not having to spend much time with the friars. The entire household was shocked and the dinner ended abruptly.

This was but a foretaste of what would come from this self-confident and irreverent servant of the Crown once he was established in Santa Fe, his behavior upsetting many in the province.

Who was he?

He came from a distinguished Spanish family. His father was from the Basque country of Spain, a neighbor of the famous Oñate family, and a Knight of the Order of Santiago, meaning an accomplished and admired soldier. He went on to hold positions of great authority across the ocean in New Spain and there married a well-placed woman of New World birth.

Their son, Bernardo López de Medizábal, was born in Mexico and attended a Jesuit college, where he studied theology with an ambition of becoming a priest. He did take minor orders, but he did not enter the priesthood, instead attending the university in Mexico City.

Later, López moved to Havana where he entered naval service, then to an administrative post in Cartagena in present-day Colombia where he found his wife, Doña Teresa, daughter of the governor. He held several other posts of importance before being appointed governor of New Mexico in 1658. He was, it was presumed, a faithful Catholic, a loyal and responsible servant of the King of Spain, and he had a justifiable sense of his own station in life.

Just why he antagonized the Franciscans is not entirely known, though (just for starters) Jesuits and Franciscans were often competitive in the missionary business. It was French Jesuits who, almost a continent away, were at the time plying Canadian rivers in Huron canoes and learning the local languages (as the Franciscans rarely did). Typically the two orders held each other in less than high regard, Jesuits being the super intellects given to logic, while the Franciscans in New Mexico were from a more penitential order and depended more on the power of poverty and penitence. Clearly Don Bernardo had absorbed much of the Jesuits' fondness for logic and debate and just as clearly he was not given to bouts of penitential fervor.

## Politics versus Religion—Again

On the caravan north in 1658 and 1659 came, as well, Fray Juan Ramírez, recently appointed as procurator-general, meaning that he was in charge of both the logistics of the journey and the Franciscans in New Mexico. He would take command of the Franciscan custodia, headquartered near the pueblo of Santo Domingo. Ramírez was from a humble background but well educated, also having studied with the Jesuits before becoming a Franciscan.

It could have been that the upper-crust Governor López was snooty about Ramírez's origins and maybe he thought it a bit traitorous for a Jesuit student to switch to the Franciscans. Maybe it was simpler (or more complicated) than that, but the two regularly quarreled during the long trip north. (Must one imagine these arguments taking place with the governor peering though the curtains of his covered wagon while the procurator-general stood outside in the hot sun and dust?)

López evidently complained that Ramírez skimped on the care he provided the governor and his wife during the long journey, and accused the Franciscan of having tried earlier to undermine

Shield design with
Maltese cross

López's very appointment. Also, it turned out, ten of the twenty-four friars on the caravan north deserted along the way, and presumably made their way back to Mexico City. Ramírez and López held each other responsible for these defections.

The two argued mostly about the authority of the friars over the lives of the Native people, the spiritual side of New Mexican life in general, and the authority of the governor over all things in the province including, ultimately, the friars and all their works. Whatever personal animosity the two held for each other—and no disagreement seems petty to people thrown together on an uncomfortable six-month trek through dangerous, difficult, and monotonous territory—the two antagonists did disagree over this all-important matter of policy. No doubt the Jesuit-trained governor felt just as comfortable as the procurator-general in these arguments in throwing around the canonical esoterica of the Church.

At any rate, by the time Fray Juan was dropped off at the Franciscan headquarters and the pack train reached Santa Fe on July 11, the battle lines were irrevocably drawn. As was the custom, Fray Juan soon officially presented himself at the Governor's Palace in Santa Fe (it was about a day's walk from Santo Domingo to the provincial capital). López broke custom and provided none of the pomp and ceremony that normally attended such an occasion. In the world of the Spanish *and* the Pueblo people, ceremony was a major form of communication. Ceremonies of all kinds certified the rightness of things and kept societies from spinning off into perilous and unknown realms of behavior. So López's unenthusiastic welcome of Fray Juan Ramírez was not merely a personal rudeness, it was an unmistakable, calculated public announcement that the governor held the office of the province's major religious figure—and therefore the missionary enterprise as a whole—in little more than contempt. Some would say that it all boiled down to a labor dispute.

## *The Inspection Tour*

About four decades earlier, the Viceroyalty of New Spain had decreed that for their labor the Pueblo Indians were to be paid half a *real* per day plus food. At the time, two and a half bushels of corn was worth four *reales* and a slave boy fetched about 250 *reales* (or thirty pesos). Before long, the rations were dropped from this pay, and in many cases the half-*real* failed to materialize either. Most likely at the behest of the government in New Spain, Governor López announced a rate increase—to a full *real* per day plus a day's rations.

The colonists reacted with a predictable outrage. This increase in the minimum wage, they complained, would make the colonists' lives impossible, putting the utterly necessary Indian labor for herding and harvesting far beyond their means. To make matters worse, the governor also began moving against those colonists who had gotten in the habit of building on Pueblo land and insisting on free Indian labor, both of which were illegal under Spanish law but "perks" some colonists had long taken for granted.

To make matters even worse, the region had recently entered a period of severe drought. Livestock production declined, and according to one report the Indians were subsisting on wild plants like spider weed. Settlers, the report said, had only spinach, bran, and various herbs to eat. López forbade the export of livestock to the south and, in raising the minimum wage, reasoned that if the colonists could no longer afford Indian labor, the Indians would have the time to see to their own sustenance. Here López betrayed what would turn out to be a consistent bias in favor of the Pueblo Indians.

Far more perilous for the friars, though, was López's ruling that the many mission jobs such as cook and bell-ringer—long filled by Indians at no pay whatsoever—now were to be paid at the full rate of one *real* per day plus rations. The friars, penurious by oath, were outraged. In fact, the law in this instance was ambiguous, even murky, but López interpreted it in a way that was consistent with his pro-Pueblo bias.

In October, López de Mendizábal began the tour of the province that was required of each new governor and, along the way, he further outraged the Franciscans who accompanied him, already deeply suspicious of López and his schemes. On a crisp fall day in the southern pueblo of Alamillo, for example, he sat bespectacled at a table in the middle of the plaza and summoned the soldiers and the Indians to come before him to answer some questions. One can readily imagine the Pueblos gathered around in the dusty plaza in the thin autumn light, with children and teenagers watching from the surrounding rooftops.

One question López asked the Indians that day was whether they supported the mission. Even before the tour had begun, the friars had insisted to all who would listen that the governor was out to embarrass them. This wholly uncalled-for question in Alamillo, a leading question if there ever were one, was proof.

López later claimed that with this line of questioning he was trying to establish a clear distinction between sins against the Church and crimes against the state. So he did go on that afternoon to ask if any friars had taken concubines and if so, had they been punished for this offense. Such, López claimed, should be considered a crime against the state, since it interfered with the rights of Indians, and therefore would be punished by the secular authorities.

Whether or not some Franciscans violated their oath of celibacy is controversial. Surely it happened from time to time, and some historians agree that in this remote (and boring) place the colonists and others had little to do for entertainment besides having a lot of sex. One later visitor to New Mexico in this era—another Franciscan—reported matter-of-factly that every pueblo had at least one child that looked a lot like the resident friar.

In their own defense, the Franciscans said the governor openly encouraged the Indians to speak out against their priests. For example, at Alamillo a woman announced that the resident friar had deflowered her. López immediately ordered a soldier to go to the priest where he sat in his room, take away his *manta* (robe), and give it to the woman as payment. The people in the plaza all laughed uproariously, the story went, while this transaction was completed. The crowd knew what López didn't. The friar in question, Fray Francisco Acevedo, was ninety years old. Given their sense of humor, the Indians surely tittered that such a deflowering would have to have been one of the Christian God's miracles.

Meanwhile the Franciscans insisted that only priests could discipline priests, but López argued that it was a civil offense, which, had he not made it public, would have given him a bad conscience for not fulfilling his gubernatorial duties. As for poor old Fray Francisco, he remained in his room, humiliated, telling his fellow friars who came to him that his defense would consist only of his age and his reputation as a holy man. He would otherwise remain silent.

The governor's inspection tour continued and by its end all the friars in New Mexico considered him an enemy of the Church. Claims and counterclaims would henceforth fly over New Mexico like bats in the night, filling the air. López had openly encouraged the Indians to do no work at the missions unless the friars paid them. And if all this were not seditious enough, López committed an unspeakable affront against what the Franciscans held as central to their holy work. He encouraged the Pueblos to resume performing their dances, including the katsina dances, openly, in their plazas, for anyone to see.

On one occasion, for example, when the governor observed a Pueblo dance held at his request, he said that it was nothing more than "Indian nonsense," no more meaningful than the folk dances of Mexico City, little more than an exercise in agility. He listened to the chanting, which in fact is a song with lyrics that to the unpracticed ear sound like little more than "heya, heya, heya." Evidently López looked over to those who were watching the dance and said, "Look there, this dance contains nothing more than this 'Hu, hu, hu,' and these thieving friars say that it is superstitious."[22]

Chances are that Don Bernardo López, an experienced administrator and student of theology, knew there was more to the Indian dances than he said. And the chances are that he actively encouraged the Pueblos to do their dances openly not just to annoy the friars but because he perceived that their prohibition was a primary source of the tension that constantly threatened the province. He was, after all, responsible for the physical safety of everyone present in New Mexico, and particularly the Hispanic settlers who were vastly outnumbered by the Pueblo Indians and subject, as well, to frequent raids by the surrounding Apaches.

Of course the friars saw it differently: To permit the dances was to undermine in the most direct way the very purpose of the colony—converting heathens and maintaining converts in their new beliefs. It was to give authority back to the devil-worshipping traditionalist sorcerers and to invite a beastly reversion to the sexual practice the friars had convinced themselves were part of every katsina dance. Decades of hard work suppressing the evil habits and rites of the barbarians were thus cavalierly thrown out the window.

### Franciscan Vengeance

To inflame the friars even further (if that were possible), López continued to accuse the friars themselves of failing to observe their solemn vow of chastity, of consorting with both Native and Hispanic women. He accused several friars of outright rape, and in one instance (in Taos) of not only raping a Pueblo woman but then murdering her to keep the incident quiet. It was common knowledge that Franciscan flesh was sometimes weak. Why the friar at Taos would have gone to such an extreme to hush up his encounter is a mystery that suggests a bit of malicious exaggeration on the part of his accuser.

In the face of these accusations, the Franciscans went into vengeance mode. They collected every bit of evidence they could to discredit Don Bernardo and to show that he, like so many of his predecessors in the Governor's palace, was an immoral, philandering, profiteering, anti-Church criminal, and probably a Judaist to boot. Indeed, for many of the charges brought against him, Don Bernardo provided ample ammunition. Whatever else the governor was, he was no saint.

To begin with, the governor and his first lady, Doña Teresa, had some disturbing habits in their private lives (which of course became instant fodder for gossip, surely via the servants). They slept without an attendant in their bedroom. They did not attend mass or even respond to pious greetings by their servants. Doña Teresa kept her writing desk locked and occasionally read from a book she kept locked up in it. Once, it was alleged, when a black servant made a pious comment, she had her whipped. The gubernatorial couple had a suspicious cleanliness hang-up, bathing every Friday, the day, it was pointed out darkly, that preceded the Jewish Sabbath.

(Jews were not welcome in Spain or Spanish colonies, having been ejected by the Crown in 1492. It turned out that many Spanish Jews did wind up covertly in the New World colonies, and after a long time and many generations, many of them forgot their Jewish heritage altogether, though some did keep on with certain simple and eventually inexplicable household ceremonies. It was only in the last few decades of the twentieth century that a significant number of old New Mexico families learned that they were at least in part Jewish.)

Doña Teresa also engaged in magical practices, treating the soles of her feet with onions, for example, and using potions that included her own menstrual blood—surely something learned from local Indian witches.

The latter ritual, it was suspected, was to improve her attractiveness to her husband, who was a philanderer reputed to go after anyone in a skirt—Pueblo woman, mestiza servant, settler's wife. López never denied such accusations but confessed to numerous affairs with single and married women, one of whom gave birth to a child. At least in López's worldview, adultery had little to do with whether or not a man loved his wife, and López was devoted to his. No wonder Doña Teresa used love potions, which she could have learned about from any Native healer or Hispanic *curandera*.

Besides undermining the missionaries and shamelessly philandering (suggesting a convenient double standard on his part), López brought accusations upon himself by engaging in entrepreneurial schemes that looked a bit fishy even in those days in New Mexico when every governor was something of a buccaneer. The pay for governor—about two thousand pesos a year—had not changed since the 1620s, and it was hardly enough to maintain a proper gubernatorial household, much less to make what amounted to exile in New Mexico worth the effort. Like his predecessors, López intended to make money and he went about it imaginatively. For example, he established a store in the Governor's Palace where he sold various necessities he had brought with him on the wagon train north—and at prices that some said amounted to gouging.

López had accused the friars of amassing large herds (and with inappropriately free Indian labor) for sale in the provinces to the south for profits that they had abjured in their vow of poverty. Also he forbade the sale of livestock to ameliorate the effects of the drought. But then he proceeded to amass his own herds for sale later. Worse yet, having raised the wages of the Indians beyond what the settler could afford, with the spoken desire that the Indians be left to improve their own crops and herds, he then hired some eight hundred of them. And for what? To accompany forty soldiers into Apache country.

López said that the Navajo Apaches had not come in to make peaceful noises to the new governor as was customary, and that furthermore he later received intelligence that they were poised to attack one or another of the pueblos. So he arranged for a pre-emptive strike. The few soldiers and the several hundred Pueblo auxiliaries attacked and returned with some seventy Navajos, chiefly women and children, which López claimed as his own and said he would sell as slaves in the south in the market town of Parras. The Franciscans counterclaimed that López made up the bit about the intelligence out of whole cloth and used it as a pretext to mount an unwarranted and illegal attack on the Navajos, then at peace, to obtain slaves to sell. This, the Franciscans said, was a violation of longstanding Spanish laws about what constituted a just war, and it was only in a just war that slaves could be taken.

Continuing the litany of crimes, the Franciscans said in reports to the officers of the Inquisition in Santo Domingo and in Mexico City, that the Navajo slaves—along with products like weavings López had forced the Indians to make for him—were delivered to the south in carts he had made the Indians build for him. Once the Indians reached the market, they were instructed to sell the cart as well. The earnings from these sales were therefore all illegally obtained, and furthermore López's actions had led to the loss of some eight thousand animals from mission herds.

## Provincial Inquisition

All these charges—a list of 132 individual counts—were brought against López and his wife before the head of the provincial Inquisition in Santo Domingo in 1660. The governor was arrested and jailed at the convent there, as was Doña Teresa—in a separate cell—where they remained for several months until transportation to Mexico City was arranged. As López was being shackled in a cart (while his wife was confined to one of the ex-governor's carriages), he evidently accused the friars of imprisoning him. But he was told that it was the Inquisition that was responsible and he replied, "Such a thing has never happened except to a God Man and now to me. I swear to Christ that I am a better Christian than all the men in the world. Look, gentlemen, there is no longer God or a King, since such a thing could happen to a man like me."[23]

This incoherent and sacrilegious outburst suggests that Don Bernardo was suffering from some sort of mental disturbance. It could possibly have been a condition that first began, however unnoticeably, during his time in the tropical lowlands of Cartagena. He did suffer from gout and evidently from typhus and a number of other physical ailments. In any event, it does suggest a seriously confused mind, and as the caravan set out for the south, Don Bernardo was surely a seriously ill man.

Once the ex-governor and (separately) Doña Teresa arrived in Mexico City, the charges were aired again and López was able to respond to them through lawyers, which he did forcefully, almost arrogantly, and with considerable effect. Eventually most of the charges were dropped and as punishment for those that had stuck, he was barred from holding any office for eight years and instructed to pay for the loss of the Franciscan herds and some other debts. But this reprieve, if it could be called such, was too late. Before the trial was over and he received his sentence, he had died.

Doña Teresa was eventually acquitted and, after two years of languishing in an Inquisition cell, was given her freedom. López's remains, which had been interred in the prison yard without ceremony, were exhumed once his trial ended and re-interred in a proper cemetery. Meanwhile, another governor, appointed while López was in the hands of the Inquisition, sought to take control of López's ill-gotten gains that had been frozen in New Mexico. Doña Teresa carried on a long legal battle over the estate and, finally unsuccessful, disappeared from the historical record.

### *Franciscan Order Restored*

Once again the tragic, violent, and murky realm of New Mexico had dashed dreams, destroyed reputations, and brought another governor down into an earthly perdition. And what had this once promising administrator, with his evident affection for the Pueblo people, this prickly, educated, outrageous, perhaps somewhat mad (and possibly uniquely modern), governor achieved?

To begin with, whatever the real reason behind López's raid on the Navajo Apaches was—preemptive strike or just a blatant slave raid—it did nothing for relations between the surrounding Apache people and the Pueblos and settlers. Sudden violent raids on the pueblos became more frequent, to the province's considerable disadvantage. The Pueblo Indians would become less and less capable of resisting these onslaughts, losing women, children, and valuable stores of food. In the complex gyre of frontier relations, when the Pueblos did not have enough reserves of corn and beans to trade to the Apaches for meat and hides, then the Apaches had to raid the pueblos for whatever they could take. It was perfectly logical.

After decades of possibly successful Franciscan indoctrination of the Indians and two full decades teaching children to speak Spanish and follow the Cross, López had significantly undermined the friars' authority in the eyes of their flocks. In 1660, Fray Juan Ramírez, who had helped manage the Franciscan onslaught against López, heard from an Isleta man that "The Indians are totally lost, without faith, and without devotion to the Church. They neither respect nor obey their ministers."[24]

On the other hand, one cannot conceive of the joy, pleasure, and relief that many of the Pueblo Indians must have felt when, once again, they were dancing, receiving the benign katsina spirits in the sunlight, and freely singing prayers into the world—making the world whole again.

López's "emancipation" of the Pueblo rites, however, produced severe blowback. The Franciscans were now doubly determined to root out any apostasy, and to regain their power over Pueblo affairs—both spiritual and secular. Individual governors came and went, typically after a few years, but the presence of the Franciscan Order was a permanent part of New Mexico. The friars would now see to it that no new governor interfered with their sacred mission. Indeed, no governor, after Don Bernardo López de Mendizábal's total humiliation, would dare go up against the intimidating power of the friars' Inquisition. And without a doubt, the Franciscans would do their utmost to put an end to the "hated and diabolical rites" that the Indians, it seemed, had not yet forgotten. If some friars had looked the other way in years past while the Indians danced in hiding, none would henceforth be so tolerant.

Not only had López temporarily lightened the Indians' toil on behalf of the colonists and the friars, but in permitting the dances to take place at all, and publicly as well, he bestowed some degree of honor and respect once again on the traditional religious leaders—a respect that might have diminished (at least in some minds) when the ceremonies had to be held in hiding, and the friars seemed to be in charge and exercising even magical powers. But it was a deep-seated Pueblo tradition that a leader was supposed to maintain peace among his people. Pueblo opponents of Christianity could ask, Where was the peace that the friars were supposed to maintain? The fissures between Pueblo factions—converted and traditional—that existed in most pueblos were all the wider now. Alliances of those against the Spanish, and those in league with them, were growing ever more complex.

# CHAPTER 9

# *The Faces of Resentment*

THE CASE CAN BE MADE that truly scientific archaeology in America began in 1915 when Alfred V. Kidder undertook the excavation of Pecos pueblo, which had been abandoned in the mid-nineteenth century, its last members moving in with their Towa-speaking relatives at Jemez. Kidder's work at Pecos lasted fourteen years. He uncovered the various forms and designs of pottery and used them to establish the sequence of human habitations in that part of the American Southwest during the past two thousand years. Southwestern Native American pottery soon became one of the most studied accumulations of artifacts anywhere on earth, providing generations of students with a window on the changes—some say the evolution—of prehistoric cultures that led to the Pueblo cultures in the sixteenth century. In that time, and earlier, each of the pueblos had developed distinctive design traditions within the larger traditions of their language mates in other pueblos.

The designs, invented and executed by women, who (so far as it is known) made all pueblo pottery, were not just pretty bits of art. They were a continuing statement of group (or tribal) identity. From the pottery designs produced in the first seventy or so years of Spanish occupation, archaeologists have recently been able to read at least some of the more subtle native reactions to that occupation.

After the first few years of the Spanish presence, once their fine clothes had worn out and whatever utensils they had had broken, the colonists took to wearing Indian-style deerskin clothes and commissioning pottery and other useful items from the Pueblo women, including some pottery in different shapes from what was traditional among the Indians.

One of the motifs that would make the Spanish happy to see on a pot was, of course, a cross, the nearly ubiquitous symbol of the Church, of Christ, and of the all-important concept of Christian redemption. And many of the Pueblo potters obliged, adorning many pots with crosses. This suggested graphically to any Spaniard, and particularly any friar who looked, that the potter was happily ensconced in the arms of the Church.

At the same time, that very same cross motif was used by Pueblo potters to represent that common and greatly admired habitué of standing water, the dragonfly, with its long tail and its quadruple wings. By putting the dragonfly into the "wrong" design context on a pot, the potter was satisfying the friars who saw crosses but at the same time, in an essentially humorous way, letting the Pueblo people know that the potter not only retained her old traditional beliefs on behalf of her people, but also was pulling wool over the eyes of the friars.

Archaeologists have found that Rio Grande Pueblo women did the same thing with other cross-like design motifs, such as stars and birds that had been in use in earlier times with other meanings, but now became distinctly more common. Similarly, to the west in Zuni, potters who had once painted images of the katsinas in the interior of bowls, now greatly simplified them, recognizably katsinas to the Zunis but simply meaningless abstractions to the friars. Another motif that suddenly became popular among Zuni potters was an array of feathers. To the friars, these were just feathers, handsome objects of no particular meaning. But the friars were unaware that feathers, and in particular eagle feathers, were highly sacred ritual objects in the worldview of the Pueblo people and that fringes of feathers were often components of ritual costume.

*Double-bar crosses. Dragonflies could be used to please the friars.*

Subversive pottery design may seem to be resistance in a very low key. Yet it was a regular, even daily reminder over the years—indeed, a visible and unforgettable assertion—of who the Pueblo people truly were and who they intended to remain. Scholars call this form of resistance—as well as the practice of traditional rites away from the view of the Franciscans—"passive" resistance. However, highly active resistance was common, and as the years went by it became more common. Over the decades, small and large explosions of violence occurred. Uprisings by a few angry Pueblo people, or by entire pueblos, had resulted in the deaths of a considerable number of Franciscans. The Spanish authorities responded with force to most of these events, hanging or otherwise executing the perpetrators. Such mini-uprisings never worked—at least not for long.

A broader-based, multi-pueblo revolt almost erupted in the early 1650s, involving the middle Rio Grande pueblos of Isleta, Alameda, San Felipe, and Cochiti, along with some of the nearby Apaches, but even this alliance was insufficient. The leaders were discovered before the uprising got off the ground, and they were summarily hanged as traitors to the Crown. It is safe to say, however, that each failed uprising became part of an accumulating wisdom among the Pueblos—food for the growth of a strategy.

Among the lessons the Pueblo rebels would have to learn was the need for large numbers, for unity among disparate peoples, and for absolute secrecy. Angry Pueblos would imagine that the right time would—might—present itself when these conditions and others were met. Meanwhile, resentment and resistance had many faces. Looking back from today on the decade or so that preceded the Pueblo Rebellion, it is difficult to imagine what could have happened that would have prevented it.

Yet another requirement for rebellion—passing information, complaints, and plans back and forth among previously standoffish Pueblos—was being greatly facilitated by some of the tragic events causing the overall Pueblo population to diminish with startling rapidity: smallpox and other disease outbreaks, periods of famine, and increased raiding.

By 1668, Spanish stores of food were being tapped and were soon exhausted. The Rio Grande itself was virtually dry. In 1670, the Spanish and the Indians were driven to eating "the hides that they had and the straps of the carts, preparing them for food by soaking and washing them and roasting them in a fire with maize, and boiling them with herbs and roots."[25]

In an isolated instance of violence, in 1672, Apaches, with the collusion of the anti-Christian Zunis, killed the resident Franciscan, Fray Pedro de Ávila y Ayala, and destroyed the church.

### Desolation and Hard Times

Drought continued well into the 1670s and pueblos continued to fail, particularly those in the southern part of the province. The Tompiro pueblos were among the worst off. In one, called Humanas, some four hundred and fifty people died of famine in one year. By 1677, the entire Tompiro region had lost its missionaries, and its pueblos were abandoned by at least a thousand families in all. The Tano villages (those lying to the south of Pecos) were similarly struck.

Many survivors of raids and disease left their home pueblos and, as refugees, moved in with others, bridging some of the gaps between language and cultural groups, sharing rituals, lessons, and resentments. Traditional leaders with long memories would surely have kept the embers of distrust and dismay over the Spanish insults glowing.

In the meantime, with the abandonment of so many pueblos, the associated Spanish encomenderos were eliminated, creating severe cuts in the numbers of men—soldiers and Indian auxiliaries—to oppose raiders who themselves were desperate from drought. Indeed, it was the Apaches who delivered the final blows to the Tompiro pueblos. Life had become an ongoing gyre of woe and desperation.

The social fabric of the pueblos was strained as never before. The population was dropping, with family and clan members dying off. The elderly (experience) and the young (hope) would usually succumb first to the mysterious onslaughts of diseases that were surely seen as impelled by witchcraft, the exercise of evil powers by *someone*—who knew whom? Was it the Spanish, who seemed immune to the plagues, or was it intramural jealousy and hate?

The glue that held traditional pueblo societies together was disappearing. Clan obligations, the faith in one's kin, the courtesies due one another, the traditional ways that had invested the community with vibrancy and strength—all this was under assault. It is possible that as some of the Pueblo holy men and women aged and died, the special ceremonies they performed were lost with them. Such spiritual losses can lead to factional hostilities even today. In addition, in a pagan, or animist, world where everything from the wind to a drop of dew is alive, the lack of rain was not a matter of blind physics and meteorology. It could be explained only with reference to the expectations of the spirit world. As a result, suspicions intensified between truly converted Pueblos and those who may have paid lip service to the Cross while retaining their traditional beliefs.

To make matters even worse, the governors in the 1670s recognized the need for solidarity in the face of increased Apache raids and the continuing recalcitrance of the Pueblos, and for the first time in a long time the civil authorities happily contributed soldiers to accompany the friars in their raids on the kivas. They assisted in the collection of ceremonial objects and helped build the piles of sacred objects in the plazas and set them on fire while Pueblo men, women, and children watched in horror. A katsina mask today, as it surely was then, is considered alive.

## Causes for Revolution

Practically all historians agree that the Pueblo Rebellion was impelled by the continuing destruction of traditional life—in most accounts, a struggle for the right to exercise their religion without interference. But this meant a great deal more to the Pueblo people than just the katsina dances. What the Spanish did not understand was that the entire Pueblo way of life—polygamy, more open sexual practices, gendered use of space in and around the pueblos, the communal nature of society—all this and more were part of their religious worldview. What the men did in the cornfields was not something separate from what they did in the kivas. Even in the nearly all-encompassing Spanish Catholicism, there was a distinction between the sacred and the secular (a distinction that Don Bernardo López de Mendizábal had sought to sharpen). No such distinction was made by the Indians. That the chief motivation for the rebellion was "religious" in the Indian sense goes without saying.

A few historians have emphasized other features of colonial domination as the direct impetus for rebellion. Ralph Emerson Twitchell, an early twentieth-century lawyer and historian, pointed to the forced labor imposed on the Pueblo people by both the secular government and the friars. This, he suggested, finally became intolerable when a series of external events—raids by Apaches and drought, primarily—occurred at once in the 1670s. Yet another historian of the rebellion—Andrew Knaut (when he was at Duke University in the 1990s)—said that the Spanish authorities, secular and religious, lost control of the pueblo Indian population because many Pueblos were in fact Hispanics.

Oñate's original plan for managing the colony was to keep colonists and Indians separate—as little in each others' lives as possible. But intermarriage was inevitable, and by the mid-century, the Pueblos with Hispanic blood in their veins also had very revealing experiences with the Spanish. They knew a great deal about how the Spanish—soldiers, governors, colonists, and friars—thought and how they lived their lives. Many had learned to manage horses. Many more, drafted into service as auxiliaries, had learned the strategies and tactics of the Spanish military. Indeed, the Spanish were busy, however unwittingly, teaching the Pueblos how to revolt.

Another contributing factor, not emphasized as much as it should be, is the nearly total dysfunction of Spanish governance. The constant stream of re-placement governors—each charged with checking up on the misdeeds of his predecessor in a formal review called the *residencia*—seems almost slapstick in retrospect. Every three years or so, a new governor showed up on the pack train, needing on-the-job training and no doubt dreading the assignment to this benighted and impoverished wasteland. The entire governmental structure in Spanish New Mexico made most disputes—small or great—irresolvable, and made one degree or another of larcenous behavior on the part of the governors (and others) a necessity. And few among this parade of men were paragons of rectitude.

For example, the man who succeeded Don Bernardo López de Mendizábal was hardly an improvement. Diego Dionisio de Peñalosa was as great a womanizer as his predecessor, which upset the friars. He was as determined to amass a fortune as was Don Bernardo, including his drawn-out effort to snatch Don Bernardo's considerable fortune in skins, livestock, and other riches away from the long-suffering Doña Teresa. If Peñalosa's transgressions were a bit milder than Don Bernardo's, his fate was much the same. He wound up in disgrace, fired from ever holding an administrative post, and expelled from New Spain altogether. Unable to return to his native Peru (where he was a criminal fugitive from a charge of official misconduct while serving as an alcalde), he decamped first to England and then France, seeking a consulting job to aid Spain's enemies in their efforts to push the Spanish out of some of their New World holdings. He soon died in France.

By this time, several families had gained prominence in New Mexico, having acquired relative wealth and lifetimes of experience living in such a strange place that had been home to them for about three generations. One such man was Juan Domínguez de Mendoza, who held a long list of administrative and military positions in the province, hopeful of one day serving as governor. Yet Domínguez de Mendoza and other natives were always overlooked by the Viceroys in Mexico City. It apparently never occurred to them to install someone who already knew the problems and the possibilities of the province. Mendoza died quixotically in Madrid, still seeking an appointment to the governorship of the province of his birth.

So it was always newcomers in the governor's palace, men who were probably as interested in Pueblo life as women in modern Libya are interested in the National Football League. And it is little wonder that—given the built-in antagonisms and the endless complaints of the colonists—New Mexico was, politically, a partisan nightmare, increasingly unable to cope with the droughts, raids, and other calamities that befell the pueblos in this period. That the Spanish had proved to be almost totally incompetent was surely a driving factor in the desperate Pueblos' need for change.

None of these reasons for rebellion are mutually exclusive. They were all surely factors of importance. It would be surprising if there were not multiple reasons to resent so intrusive an occupying force, especially one that sought to eliminate the local way of life almost totally. Perhaps the least persuasive reason suggested by a few historians is that the Pueblos and the Hispanics and Franciscans all got along pretty well for the most part over the decades until the mid-1670s. Many of the Pueblo Indians had converted and seemed faithful enough, accepting the religious and other obligations. Most of the Pueblos, this view maintains, had accommodated themselves to the Spanish occupation and were living a new way of life—part Indian, part Spanish. This is probably so. The Pueblos were using many Spanish tools and techniques, and eating foods introduced by the Spanish. The colonists and the Pueblos were sharing agricultural and other practices, including folk medicines. According to this view, the disastrous drought period and the resulting famine led the Pueblo people to rise up in desperation, not so much in dissatisfaction with Spanish ways but a general dissatisfaction with the state of things.

This scenario is not valid for several reasons, chief of which is that if the Pueblos were comfortable with Christianity, why would they rise up and torture and kill the very embodiments of the Catholic faith—the friars who had converted them and fed them in times of dire straits for as long as the missions' stores held out?

## Precursor to War

In the spring of 1675, a rebellion erupted from San Ildefonso in Tewa country, spreading to several other Tewa villages. The rebels attempted to "bewitch" one of the Franciscans and a couple of Spaniards, along with murdering others. Governor Juan Francisco Treviño reacted speedily and with a maximum of impact. He ordered his soldiers to assist the Franciscans on a major roundup of the Pueblo religious leaders—sorcerers—in the Tewa and other pueblos. Led by mounted officers, the soldiers stormed into the pueblos, commandeered the plazas, and in the rising dust and terror hauled the religious leaders out of their adobe houses into the sun.

One by one, the old religious leaders/medicine men from the central region of Spanish dominion were captured—in all, forty-seven of them. Treviño had given orders that four of these individuals be executed and three were promptly hanged—one of them in Jemez, another in San Felipe (one of the Keres pueblos), and the other, a Tewa, in the pueblo of Nambe. The fourth spared the Spanish the effort and hanged himself. The rest of the men—deemed conspirators though they could not all have been involved in the San Ildefonso uprising—were publicly flogged and thrown in prison in Santa Fe.

Among the imprisoned forty-three was a religious figure from the pueblo that was known by the Spanish as San Juan, the site where the Rio Grande and the Rio Chama meet and where Juan de Oñate had established his first colonial headquarters seventy-seven years earlier. Smoldering in outrage among his brutalized and humiliated colleagues, this man from San Juan went by the name of Po'pay. In good time, he would wreak a very certain vengeance.

# PART TWO

# CALAMITY

# CHAPTER 10

# *Preparing for Rebellion*

THE WHOLESALE ARREST and humiliation of forty-seven spiritual leaders of the pueblos in 1675 may well have been the tipping point leading to the Pueblo Revolt. We think of tipping points as those events that *immediately* lead to the major event, but the Pueblo rebels still had a lot to accomplish once the fatal decision was made.

The day after the mass humiliation of Pueblo religious leaders, a delegation of some seventy Tewa warriors showed up in Santa Fe, demanding an audience with Governor Juan Francisco Treviño, and this too could be considered the tipping point. The warriors had come to negotiate for the release of the medicine men. They crowded into the governor's quarters in the wooden and adobe buildings called *Casas Reales*, the government headquarters.

It must have been an alarming moment for the governor, having his palace overrun with seventy men bearing weapons, streaks of paint, and a deep-seated anger. They brought with them eggs and chickens, beans, tobacco, and some small deerskins, as negotiating gifts. The angry warriors likely outnumbered the Spanish soldiers present in Santa Fe that day, and even more warriors stood in reserve in the surrounding hills.

Treviño handed out some blankets (traditional gifts) to his visitors and suggested that they put aside their grievances. The warriors said that if Treviño did not release the prisoners from captivity, they would simply kill him. Faced with this choice, Treviño perhaps wisely decided not to join any of the Franciscans in martyrdom. Instead, he told the Tewas, "Wait a while, children, I will give them to you and pardon them on condition that you forsake idolatry and iniquity."[26]

The warriors would have none of that. They continued to insist on the release of the medicine men, and in this war of threats Treviño blinked. The Spaniards, it was now clear, were not invincible.

The Pueblo leaders, many of them still burning with resentment over the most recent outrage, were soon released and returned to their pueblos. The Tewa warriors had achieved a remarkable victory and had uncovered a seam of weakness in the Spanish government. The governor himself had backed down and given in. To achieve this victory, the Tewa warriors had also acted in a pan-pueblo manner. Many of the men released from Spanish imprisonment were Tewas, but many spoke Keres, Towa, and other tongues.

At some point soon after the forty-three were released, the man called Po'pay left his home pueblo of San Juan to escape harassment from Francisco Xavier, the thuggish secretary of government and war. He went to Taos, farther from the center of Spanish influence and a place where sympathy for rebels was longstanding. He evidently persuaded the Taos leaders to turn over to him a kiva in which he could lay his plans. He was, it turned out, a remarkably persuasive man.

Po'pay was also, evidently, a person of shamanic skills. Shamans are reputed to enter the world of spirits—both evil and benign—in order to heal people by repelling or in other ways defeating the evil spirits doing the damage. Beyond the salves and teas and other potions used in native curing, shamans around the world are held in a kind of awe, for it stands to reason that someone who can repel the spirits and forces of evil by manipulating them in one way or another, can also put those same spirits to work doing harm to people.

To this day, on many American Indian reservations and in other tribal societies, shamanistic medicine men are both sought after for help and greatly feared for their knowledge of the dark arts of witchcraft. In any case, part of Po'pay's persuasiveness must have resided in these powers.

### Failure to Act

Meanwhile, it seems that the Spaniards were in a state of what today is called denial. Not much evidence survives that they understood the degree of heat Pueblo resentment had reached. For the moment, other matters impinged daily and more directly. The drought went on relentlessly. The farther-flung pueblos were being abandoned, unleashing a small horde of refugees into the other pueblos. The Spanish government, such as it was, could not have been more overextended. Indeed, the world was falling apart.

One man seemed capable of understanding the needs and possibilities of the colony. This was Fray Francisco de Ayeta. In 1674, he had been put in charge of supplying the colony and would later be put in charge of the entire missionary effort in New Mexico. A native of Pamplona, he was an energetic man in his thir-ties at the time. Among his first actions in the province was to agree with Gover-nor Treviño and the rest of the ruling Spanish (in essence, the cabildo of Santa Fe) that more troops were needed along with their proper outfitting, in order to stem the tide of raiding by the Apaches. Fray Ayeta therefore hastened to New Spain with his petition to the Viceroy for the help for New Mexico that, as historian Kessell wrote, "neither she nor her downtrodden populace could provide."[27]

Ayeta succeeded, and set out with the triennial pack train for the north on February 27, 1677. With the usual supplies, the train brought a new governor, Antonio de Otermín, fifty soldiers (who had been convicts), a hundred harquebuses along with other weapons, saddles and horse tack, and a thousand horses. This promising pack train arrived in Santa Fe in December, 1677 (except for six of the felons who went AWOL along the way).

Not a great deal is known about Otermín, the new governor. He was a man of some military experience but he was a bit passive. He turned over many of his duties to subordinates, particularly Francisco Xavier, the field officer who had led the assault on the forty-seven medicine men in 1675 under the banner of Governor Treviño. The Pueblo people considered him "a man of bad faith, avaricious and crafty."[28]

Otermín also allowed Fray Ayeta to take an active hand in provisioning the troops as they were allocated to various pueblos such as Galisteo in the east and Senecú in the south for defense against the raiders. Hardly had he finished this task than Ayeta returned to New Spain with a request for fifty more soldiers. Just how pathetically deficient the situation was in New Mexico (not to mention New Spain) is illustrated by the thought that a hundred new soldiers, at least half of them the dregs from New Spain's prisons, were all that could be summoned to protect a colony of thirty missions beset by an unknown number of raiding Apaches and with a resident population of some seventeen to twenty *thousand* Pueblo Indians who deeply resented their Spanish masters.

But, again, the Spanish authorities, led now by the new governor, Antonio de Otermín, seemed relatively oblivious to the conspiracy that was afoot among the northern pueblos, a conspiracy centered in the Taos kiva where Po'pay communed with spirit beings who were not at all pleased with the Spanish treatment of the Pueblo people.

## Po'pay's Spiritual Strategies

In Taos, Po'pay conversed with Poseyemu, an important member of the Tewa pantheon of deities. Poseyemu was the first of the Tewa people to climb a Douglas fir that grew in a sacred lake, arriving in the current world from an earlier one. As such, he was a supernatural Tewa cultural hero who taught the people the arts of living. Po'pay sought Poseyemu's instruction about the tactics and strategy to return to the old pueblo ways, to the world before the Spaniards. Poseyemu was known by other similar names to the non-Tewa Pueblos and would have been a persuasive figure to invoke throughout the pueblo world. Po'pay's intent was to rid all the pueblos and all the land around of Spaniards. They were all to be killed and all their works destroyed.

Po'pay explained to trusted lieutenants that the ancient gods would not return with their gifts of rain, good crops, and prosperity before all the Christians and their gods, notably Mary and Jesus, were dead. He promised that only then would the Pueblos "gather large crops of grain, maize with large thick ears, many bundles of cotton, many calabashes and watermelons."[29] Whoever among them "killed a Spaniard will get a woman for his wife, and he who kills four will get four women . . ." and so on. This was to be in retribution for those who had been whipped and had their hair cut for being polygamous.

Po'pay insisted the people had to respect the katsinas. He himself was regularly visited by three katsina spirits, he said—Caudi, Tilini, and Tleume—who lived in the kiva with Po'pay but never came out. Finally, after much prayer, the three did come out, emitting fire from "all the extremities of their bodies." Having emerged from the kiva, they announced that they were going underground, to disappear in the lake of Copal until all the Spaniards were gone and their works destroyed. (Copal was, in fact, a secret lake of Spanish mythology that had migrated from New Spain to somewhere in or near New Mexico. The purity Po'pay so ferociously sought was not totally without Spanish influences.)

Just who were these three "katsinas" who stayed in the kiva with Po'pay? Alfonso Ortiz, a Tewa who trained as an anthropologist,

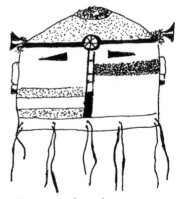

*Drawing based on Acoma mask representing Poseyemu*

pointed out that Tilini is the name of an important Tewa deity, and he supposed that the others may have been deities from two other non-Tewa pueblos. Po'pay was presumably calling on a widespread array of deities, representing all the linguistic groups to be involved, to legitimize what he would be asking the Pueblos to do.

But what about the fire emitted from their extremities? No explanation has been offered for this strange phenomenon until recently, when Peter Whitely, curator of Anthropology at The American Museum of Natural History in New York, wrote that this fits well with the typical results of using peyote, a hallucinogenic cactus that has been used in many Native American ceremonies around the continent throughout the centuries. So did Po'pay use peyote and relate his visions to others? Or did others as well use peyote and see the fires?

It could be that Po'pay (and others) were using peyote to increase the intensity of imagination that let them become such potent revolutionaries. But then again peyote does not grow in the Rio Grande valley, and there is no record or even suggestion of Pueblo people using it as an import from Mexico or Texas. But there is a similar hallucinogen common to the Rio Grande Valley and Arizona—the leafy, shrubby plant with white flowers called Jimson weed or datura. Why, however, wouldn't Po'pay and the Pueblos in general want to be hallucinogen-independent? So the fiery "katsinas" remain a mystery to this day.

The story got around among the Spanish at least that one of the figures who appeared to Po'pay in his kiva was a huge black man with yellow eyes. This led to a theory proposed by Fray Angelico Chavez, a late twentieth-century Franciscan brother, that the revolt was led not by Po'pay but by a black member of one of the Tewa pueblos named Naranjo, whose descendants still inhabit a number of Tewa pueblos today. Chavez's view was that the Pueblos were not sophisticated enough to have strategized and executed a revolt by themselves. The implication here that their ancestors were childlike does not sit well with contemporary Pueblo people. Very few people take Chavez's notion very seriously, the main explanation being that among the Pueblo people in those times there was no way a non-Indian could rise to such a position of authority.

Po'pay was a persuasive and, in many ways, scary leader. He let it be known that in addition to Poseyemu and the three katsinas now gone to the secret lake, he was often visited by demons and other dangerous spirit figures, all of whom he was commandeering for the work ahead.

Po'pay also surrounded himself with many of the leading war chiefs of the pueblos, swearing them to absolute secrecy. This was paramount, so much so that Po'pay, finding that his son-in-law, Nicolás Bua, had been appointed the Indian governor of San Juan and was friendly with the Spanish, saw to it that he was murdered. It is not clear if Po'pay had some subalterns stone Bua to death in his fields or if Po'pay himself murdered him. But no person of such holy stature as to be the religious and ultimate leader of a pueblo ever kills anyone or anything. So people have wondered exactly what position in the panoply of priesthoods Po'pay may have held. Possibly he was a war chief like most of the other conspirators, but more likely he was a leading member of a medicine society, though one given to shamanistic practices.

He was a superb organizer. He sought and gained the loyal alliance of a number of important war chiefs from around the pueblo world. Over the years before the revolt, they met often, usually at the feast days of the various pueblos. Feast days were great celebrations where people from other pueblos would come to celebrate, eat, and visit friends or relatives in the host pueblo. From time to time, bands of Apaches would show up as well, and some probably plotted with the Pueblo conspirators. In the crowds, the conspirators' presence would hardly be noticed as they perfected their plans. Part of their job was to explain to all the pueblos that the uprising would occur, and that any pueblo that decided not to join in would be sacked and destroyed along with any remnants there of Spanish occupation. The destruction, Po'pay said, would be accomplished with the help of the Apache warriors who were anxious to assist.

## *Preference for Peace*

Plenty of reasons existed for not joining up, even though the thought of being liberated was probably attractive to everyone in the pueblos. Many Pueblos simply preferred peace. While few of them were truly devoted Christians, some probably admired the friars, and many had blood ties to the Spanish. Some of the encomenderos had been helpful in times of drought and famine, and had helped protect Pueblos against the raids of the barbarian Apaches. Many simply did not want to give up the various benefits of the Spanish economy. And some wondered how the Pueblos were to defend themselves against the Apaches without Spanish soldiers and weapons. It is altogether possible that some were suspicious or downright afraid of Po'pay himself, who was hardly the avatar of the peaceful religious chief who sought harmony for his people. Some were simply scared of going along with so odd and fanatical a leader. In some pueblos, the populations were divided.

Most of the pueblos from Sandia north to Taos and the western pueblos were committed, but a few Pueblo leaders were sufficiently nervous about Po'pay and his plan that they tried to sabotage it in early August, 1680.

## Final Plans

Why that August was chosen as the time to ignite the rebellion is not known for certain. It was near the end of a three-year cycle when the pack train from New Spain would soon arrive, so the Spaniards were at their most distressed in terms of supplies of food and weaponry. Early August also was the time of year when the Rio Grande floodwaters made crossing the river down south near El Paso del Norte difficult or impossible. The new group of fifty soldiers Fray Francisco Ayeta had rounded up in New Spain would be blocked.

In early August, Po'pay and his lieutenants sent out messengers carrying knotted strings to each of the participating pueblos, with the instruction to untie one knot a day. When the last knot was untied, it was the time to strike. In each case, the last knot would be untied August 11. On August 9, however, leaders of five of the Tano pueblos—Galisteo, San Cristobal, San Lázaro, San Marcos, and La Cienega—rode to Santa Fe to alert the Spanish authorities of Po'pay's plan, and that same day two priests and the Indian alcalde mayor of Taos sent messages about the forthcoming uprising.

It is surprising that Governor Antonio de Otermín did not immediately undertake the kinds of precautions one might expect in the face of an onslaught of angry Pueblos—for example, sending small groups of soldiers out to protect as many missions as possible, or calling in the colonists to Santa Fe where they would be protected at least by large numbers rather than trying to resist attacks all by themselves. Perhaps the governor thought two days gave him plenty of time for all that. He did send word that in the event of hostilities, everyone north of Santa Fe should assemble there, while those to the south should assemble at Isleta where the lieutenant governor Alonso García was presently stationed.

On August 9, as part of the general alert to the rebellious pueblos, two young runners, Omtua and Catua, were carrying knotted strings to pueblo leaders and were captured and taken to Otermín, who had them tortured, interrogated, and subsequently executed. But before their deaths, they had convinced Otermín that the revolt would start on August 13. Learning of this, Po'pay sent other runners out to alert the Pueblo leaders that the revolt would begin on the morning of August 10, 1680, not the eleventh. And that is when old Fray Pío, seeking to calm his flock in Tesuque, became the first known casualty of the Pueblo–Spanish war of liberation.

# CHAPTER 11

# *The First Days*

ALL HELL BROKE LOOSE on the morning of August 10, 1680, and Governor Otermín would not learn the half of it for another two days.

Seventy miles north of the palace of the governor, in the valley of Taos, the men of Picuris and Taos pueblos fell upon the missionaries and the seventy Hispanic settlers there, slaughtering all of them except two, who escaped. Leaving their dead wives and children, these two finally, days later, made their way south to Isleta where the lieutenant governor, Alonso García, had gathered a large group of southern refugees and planned to lead them out of harm's way.

On the bloody first day of the revolt, in both Picuris and Taos, the Indians profaned and burned the mission churches, and plundered the fields and Spanish houses. Having taken their vengeance and collected the Spaniards' weapons and horses, the warriors headed south to Tewa country to join the rest of the uprising.

Historian Joe Sando from Jemez pueblo has written that the rebels merely wanted the Spaniards to leave the pueblo world, and asked the victims to go, killing them only when they refused. This, frankly, sounds like a bit of well-intentioned spin on Sando's part, possibly designed to soften twentieth-century Hispanic–Pueblo relations. It is hard to imagine the Indians rounding up a family of Spaniards, asking them if they would leave the province, and only then summoning up the rage to club them to death. And then doing this again and again. The fury with which the Indians of almost all the pueblos went about killing some four hundred Spaniards that day suggests that their deaths were the object all along.

In the region of the Tewa pueblos, concentrated north of Santa Fe, very few Spaniards escaped. Those who gathered at a Spanish settlement, La Cañada, not far from the Santa Clara pueblo, assembled in the house of the alcalde mayor, Luis de Quintana. Later, on August 13, they made their way through the destruction and slaughter to Santa Fe. The Tewas dispatched into martyrdom all of the missionaries at their pueblos and killed all the Spanish colonists who had not gathered at La Cañada. Then, joined by the warriors from Picuris and Taos, they moved on to begin the siege of Santa Fe.

South of Santa Fe along the Rio Grande, the Keres pueblos erupted similarly. In Santo Domingo, the Franciscan headquarters, the Indians dragged the three friars on hand out of the convent early in the morning and murdered them, their bodies being piled up before the altar in the church. Charles Hackett, whose two-volume history is the primary source of translated documents from the revolt and its immediate aftermath, writes of this horror, "it is doubtful if there could have been for the padres a sweeter death, a grander sepulcher, or a crown of martyrdom quite so coveted or so glorious as that which they earned for themselves while defending the holy faith in the convent of Santo Domingo on San Lorenzo day."[30] In all, twenty-one friars would achieve just such a glorious martyrdom in New Mexico that day.

The slaughter continued in Santo Domingo, led by Alonso Catiti, one of Po'pay's co-conspirators. None of the Spanish in the pueblo survived. Many of the Spanish had assembled at one house in a futile attempt to defend themselves against the rebels. The next day the six-mile road to San Felipe was strewn with the stripped corpses of twenty or so Spanish officers and settlers—men, women, and children.

In the pueblo of San Diego de Jemez, a daring escape worthy of the movies took place in the dark of night, involving the propitiously timed arrival of what can only be thought of as "the cavalry." Around midday of August 10, a Pueblo ambassador arrived and told Luis de Granillo, the alcalde mayor and captain of war of the Jemez and Keres pueblos, that Governor Otermín and all the Spaniards, including settlers, missionaries, women, and children, from Taos to Santo Domingo were dead. He said that even as he spoke, the Rio Abajo pueblos (meaning all the pueblos south of Santo Domingo) were being destroyed by Pueblo and Apache forces.

Granillo, one friar, and two soldiers waited until dark before fleeing on horseback, but were spotted by the rebels and chased for about five miles down the Jemez River toward the pueblo of Sia (often spelled Zia today). There they met the lieutenant governor, Alonso García, and four mounted soldiers who had received a call for aid and had set out earlier from Isleta. Seeing this, the

Pueblos gave up the chase and let them go. At Sia, four more Spaniards who were besieged in the convent, along with some livestock, escaped and joined García and Granillo.

Evidently, the Indians noticed this and sounded the alarm, shouting and ringing bells, but to no avail. The Spaniards continued downstream to Santa Ana pueblo where they found that the men had all deserted, leaving their women behind. The women told García's party "with much impudence" that their husbands had all left to kill Spaniards. And so the García party turned south and followed the Rio Grande toward Isleta and a temporary safety.

At Jemez, after Granillo and others fled, the rebels hauled Fray Juan de Jesús from his cell and took him to the cemetery, where, according to historian J. Manuel

*Mystery rock art, Frijoles Canyon*

Espinosa, "they stripped him naked, mounted him on a pig, and beat him cruelly as they ridiculed him and led him about the cemetery."[31] Then they took him off the pig and forced him to crawl around on all fours while they rode him, whipping him all the while.

"Do with me as you wish, for this joy of yours will not last more than ten years," Fray Juan is reported as saying, "after which you will consume each other in wars."[32] The Indians then beat him to death with clubs.

Meanwhile, the people of the few remaining Tano pueblos and Pecos joined the uprising, paying no heed to their leaders who had seen fit to alert Otermín. About half of the people at Pecos remained loyal to the Spaniards and the Cross, while the other faction joined the Tanos in rebellion. One reason the Pecos warriors turned against the Spanish was that the hated Francisco Xavier had recently kidnapped a group of Apaches, sending many of them south into slavery, and thus fouling relations between the Apaches and the Pecos traders. Indeed, some of the more economically minded Pueblos from Pecos blamed the uprising on Antonio de Otermín since it was he who had turned over so much of the management of the province to the vicious Francisco Xavier. The friars still resident at the Tano pueblos were killed, but the Pecos rebels did not murder their old missionary, Fray Fernando de Velasco. Instead, they sent him to Galisteo where the Tanos promptly did.

In Acoma, the two friars were bound together with an old Christian Indian woman in between, all three having been stripped naked. They were led around the pueblo while being beaten, and were finally stoned to death and thrown into a deep pit.

So it went that twenty-one friars met their deaths after being ridiculed and tortured in an explosion of rage that had been building for decades. Before the end of the uprising's first day, the sky above the Rio Grande valley was hazy with the smoke of haciendas and estancias burning, of churches and convents afire. In addition to the torture inflicted on the Franciscans in Jemez, Taos, Acoma, and elsewhere, the enraged Pueblo warriors committed the most unspeakable blasphemies upon the Cross, defecating on the altars and slathering whatever icons remained with feces. A month later, Francisco Xavier would describe the horrid acts of the "blind fiends of the devil":

> They set fire to the holy temples and images, mocking them with their dances and making trophies of the priestly vestments and other things belonging to divine worship. Their hatred and barbarous ferocity went to such extremes in the pueblo of Sandia images of saints were found among excrement, two chalices were found concealed in a basket of manure, and there was a carved crucifix with the paint and varnish taken off by lashes . . . a sculptured image of Saint Francis with the arms hacked off . . .[33]

Clearly, the attacks were as much on the Catholic religion as on its human leaders. It was in great part a religious war.

Throughout the area, horses and mules had been freed to roam—those, at least, not ridden now by Pueblo warriors. They were now in the hands of the rebels as were about one hundred harquebuses—half of all the harquebuses in the province. Warriors from virtually all the pueblos located in Río Arriba, the upper river, as well as the pueblos such as Sandia just to the south, all headed for Santa Fe where they intended to exterminate whatever Spaniards remained. They sang of the death of Jesus and Mary, and proclaimed that their own gods, whom they had never stopped worshipping, were alive and triumphant.

Far to the west, probably not on the first day of the revolt, the Acomas, Zunis, and Hopis put an end to the lives of the Franciscans in their midst. At Hopi, four Franciscans were killed. In the village of Oraibi, two members of the Badger clan took the form of warrior katsinas and knocked on the convent door. When it opened, they grabbed the friars, Fray Joseph de Espeleta and

Fray Agustín de Santa María, killed them, and threw the corpses over the side of the mesa to pile up in a martyred heap on the rocks below. The church there, as well as those in the other Hopi missions at Shongopavi and Awatovi, were destroyed, the wooden beams being kept for other uses such as shoring up the roofs of kivas. The two-hundred-pound bells, so piously hauled the thousand miles from New Spain over the years, were destroyed, except at Oraibi where they were hidden, and remain so to this day.

### Denial Overcome, Severity Understood

Seen through the fog of war and a minimum of historical documentation, these are the events of the first day of the Pueblo-Spanish War—that is, the events acted out by the Indians. But what of Governor Otermín and the Spanish officers and settlers of the province—those who escaped the slaughter?

By about five o'clock of the first day of the uprising, Governor Otermín and his officers were convinced that something deadly serious was taking place. Early that morning, Otermín had seen to it that his own jurisdiction—that is, the villa of Santa Fe—was fortified. He had sent word the day before—on the 9th—to the alcaldes mayores of the region to fortify themselves against a possible attack, and he was unaware, among other things, that such advice had not reached all districts. He believed that all the districts were taking care of themselves. In Santa Fe, per his instructions, the people of the city gathered all their weapons and assembled in the royal houses for defense. Soldiers were posted in the church to protect the holy sacrament.

At about five o'clock two soldiers from Taos appeared at the governor's palace and made a report to the governor. Nicolás Lucero and Antonio Gómez had been dispatched to inform the governor of the outbreak of violence there. On their way south, they heard a great deal about the atrocities perpetrated in the larger Tewa district. They had made their way to Santa Fe in spite of many arrows and harquebuses fired at them by the Indians in their flight through the mountains north of the capital city.

Otermín later sent out Francisco Gómez and some soldiers to ascertain how widespread the carnage was. On August 12, Gómez reported back to Otermín that some thirty deaths had occurred in Tewa country and that the Indians had fortified themselves in the pueblos of Santa Clara and Tesuque. He reported that they captured an Indian and repeatedly called on him to surrender. The Indian insisted that he would rather die and go to the Inferno, so the soldiers, obligingly, shot him.

So it would not be until August 13, the third day of the uprising, that Governor Otermín and those assembled in the royal house of Santa Fe—in all a thousand people along with livestock—would realize just how much trouble they were in. In a last move before the expected siege began, Otermín ordered the friars in Santa Fe to eat the holy sacrament at the church of San Miguel and close it down.

# CHAPTER 12

# The Siege of Santa Fe

ON AUGUST 13, two days before the siege of Santa Fe began in earnest, Otermín sent two trusted young Pueblo men with letters for the alcaldes mayores expressing his hope of discovering the extent of the damage in Tano and Keres country, on the off chance that anyone remained alive in those districts. The governor reasoned that two local Indians would have a better chance of making their way through the pockets of hostility than anyone Spanish.

Otermín had already heard that the Tano Pueblos had risen up along with some from Pecos and murdered their missionaries. This came as a grievous shock since it had been the Tano chieftains themselves who had ridden to Santa Fe on August 9 to warn of the uprising. But even as the rebellious forces began to make their way toward Santa Fe, filtering downriver and past the mountains to the north, Otermín still thought he might negotiate a way out of this calamity.

Early on the morning of August 15, around five hundred Indians gathered in the cornfields of Las Milpas de San Miguel, the plain south of the capital city, sacking the houses in the Hispanic barrio out there as they approached. Otermín sent out a small troop of soldiers to parley. At that point one of Otermín's two Pueblo messengers, Juan, the trusted Christian member of a Tano pueblo and a figure in the gubernatorial household, appeared, now mounted on horseback and decked out with a harquebus, sword, and other weaponry, and a sash of red taffeta around his waist.

The Spanish recognized the sash as stolen from the missal in the convent in Galisteo, a sorry bit of blasphemy and a clear sign of the friar's martyrdom. The Spanish soldiers persuaded Juan, now perceived not only as a traitor but as a captain of the rebellion, to enter the plaza of Santa Fe and talk to the governor.

Otermín scolded Juan for his treasonous betrayal of confidence—he, the governor himself, having made Juan a trusted member of the governor's entourage. Juan answered that it was too late, it couldn't be helped. Many Franciscans and other Spaniards had been killed, he reported, and the Indians were determined now to sack the villa and kill all the Spaniards there unless they agreed to leave the country altogether. Juan said they had brought two crosses with them, one red, the other white. If Otermín chose the red one, the siege would begin and the Spanish would all perish. If he chose the white one, the Indians would stand down while the Spaniards left the province.

Otermín elected not to choose. Instead, he instructed Juan to tell the hordes to go to their homes and he would forgive them for their treason against the Crown and for all the sacrileges they had committed. They would be able to remain Christians in good standing. By not choosing between the two crosses, Otermín had crossed his Rubicon. Juan, bedecked in his sash and Spanish weaponry, rode out of the plaza and joined the Tano and Pecos warriors on the edge of the city. They welcomed him back with shouts and the ringing of bells and, in reply to Otermín's offer of an official pardon, they set the chapel of San Miguel aflame.

The siege was on. Otermín sent a band of soldiers out to deflect the Indians, who proceeded to fight so furiously in and around the houses of the villa with weapons taken earlier from hapless Spanish settlers that the governor was forced to lead the rest of his soldiers into the fray. Of the thousand people secured in the *casas reales* (government houses), only about one hundred and twenty were capable of bearing arms. However, they put up a fight that lasted throughout the day, and killed many of the attacking Indians, though figures on casualties are hard to come by. One Spanish account suggests that about three hundred Indians were killed that first day of the siege, but this seems to be an exaggeration. Enough died, however, that the surviving Tano warriors were greatly disturbed over their losses, so much so that upon returning to their pueblo, some of them took out their rage by executing four Spanish women they had captured earlier.

No Spanish soldiers were killed during the siege that day but many were wounded. By the end of the day, the sky was dark with smoke from burning houses and the explosions of gunpowder, and the attacking Tanos were fairly soundly beaten. As they were preparing to give up the ground altogether, Tewa, Taos, and Picuris warriors appeared on the scene, and fell upon the villa from the other side (facing the mountains), forcing Otermín's men to leave.

The battle was waged sporadically through the night and the following days, with arrows and occasionally harquebus shot raining down on the settlers and livestock. On the second day, the forces confronted each other without any major hostilities taking place. The Pueblos were evidently content to wage a staring match while they waited for yet other warriors to arrive.

By the third day of the siege, warriors from Jemez had arrived and Otermín estimated that in all some 2,500 warriors confronted the few Spanish. Conditions in the casas reales and the plaza went from bad to appalling, with little to eat in the first place and the royal stores diminishing at a rapid rate, with nothing to do except cower from incoming arrows and shot. The stench arising from a thousand humans and some livestock cramped in a restricted space was overwhelming.

*Pueblo Bonito clay pipe*

Conditions grew even worse when the Indians diverted the irrigation ditch that carried water from the Santa Fe River (no deluge in the best of circumstances) into and through the plaza. Thirst was added to hunger. Without water, animals began dying, adding to the horror. Maggots and beetles did their useful ugly work. Otermín and his thousand refugees were trapped, lost, cut off from all communication with the rest of the world, while their Pueblo captors launched arrows, ignited fires, and danced with manic glee, chanting, singing that the Spanish God and Santa María were dead and gone.

Otermín wrote that this terrible time

> was the most horrible that could be thought of or imagined, because the whole villa was a torch and everywhere were war chants and shouts. What grieved us most were the dreadful flames from the church and the scoffing and ridicule which the wretched and miserable Indian rebels made of the sacred things, intoning the *alabado* and the other prayers of the church with jeers.[34]

On the 21st of August, the Spaniards recognized that the siege of Santa Fe was coming to an end—an end that meant the death of the Spanish. After all their efforts over more than eighty years to civilize this godforsaken, arid, and hopeless place, its thousands of barbarians now screaming and leaping in the shadows and the fire and smoke and profaning of the sacramental representations of the Holy Faith, Otermín's officers and noncommissioned officers of the province decided to hold a meeting.

They determined that the only satisfactory path left was to go out in glory, to sally forth from the casas reales with all of their remaining weaponry and with faith in their saints, and fight the overwhelming hordes to the death. Just what fate Otermín and his military men thought this left for the women and children while the men died on the battlefield was not reported, but it is easily imagined: slavery or death.

The next morning the mounted Spanish force charged out of the plaza and trampled a group of surprised Indians with their horses' hooves, and went on to kill three hundred Indians and capture forty-seven.

The captives were brought into the plaza, interrogated about the reasons for the revolt, and then executed. All this, of course, left the Spanish back in the casas reales without food and still facing some two thousand angry Pueblos bent on their destruction. Otermín himself was wounded, twice in the face, evidently by arrows, and once in the chest by a distant and, he thought, miraculous harquebus shot that failed to penetrate his leather vest but was nonetheless quite painful. In this siege, the Spanish had so far, by their count, killed some six hundred Indians and had lost but five soldiers, though many were wounded.

The next morning, Otermín and his thousand refugees and soldiers, some riding the few remaining horses and trusting in divine providence, walked away from Santa Fe while the Pueblos stood back and watched. Why did the Indians simply let them go? Perhaps they were sated with death, perhaps even in a state of shock. That the Spanish were leaving was now sufficient.

Otermín headed for the pueblo of Isleta where he hoped to meet up with the lieutenant governor Alonso García and whatever settlers and still-Christian Indians might still be there. When they reached the pueblo of La Alameda just north of the present-day city limits of Albuquerque, they came across an old Indian who informed them that García and all the people who had gathered at Isleta had left more than a week earlier and were on their way to El Paso del Norte.

Further south at Alamillo pueblo, Otermín demanded of another old man who had chosen to stay behind what had possessed the Pueblos to disobey both God and their King and leave. The governor then received an earful:

> [The Indians] had been plotting to rebel and kill the Spaniards and the religious, and that they had been planning constantly to carry it out, down

to the present occasion . . . He declared that the resentment which all the Indians have in their hearts has been so strong, from the time this kingdom was discovered, because the religious and the Spaniards took away their idols and forbade their sorceries and idolatries; that they have inherited successively from their old men the things pertaining to their ancient customs; and that he has heard this resentment spoken of since he was of an age to understand.[35]

Otermín sent out four horsemen to catch up with García and his party and to order them to stop. But it was clear that García had concluded that Otermín and all his refugees were dead; otherwise he would not have left his post at Isleta. And so it began to dawn on Don Antonio de Otermín, as he led a thousand bedraggled settlers and soldiers, and a handful of still faithful Christian Indians downriver toward the deserted pueblo of Isleta, that he had lost the royal province of New Mexico.

# CHAPTER 13

# A Long Walk

FOR MOST OF THE LONG WALK that Governor Antonio de Otermín then undertook, the refugees were not threatened. But they were taunted, jeered at, and mostly just watched as they struggled along past abandoned pueblos and then, to the south, Apaches. No one doubts (or doubted then) that the Indians along the way could have killed every one of the hapless Spaniards who were poorly armed, poorly clothed, hungry, and no doubt weakened from the siege and its attendant horrors. But the Indians evidently were content to see that the European intruders simply left . . . and for good.

As tragic as it was, this long walk had some nearly comedic aspects in retrospect, largely on account of the fact that there were three parties involved and none of them knew the whereabouts of the others for a good part of the time.

As we saw earlier, Otermín knew Alonso García was ahead of him somewhere south of Isleta, which Otermín and his refugees found deserted when they reached it on September 3. Otermín had no idea how many people were with García. Otermín's horsemen finally came across García at a place called Fray Cristóbal that was miles downriver, well below Isleta. Until that moment, García was of the belief that Otermín and all the Spaniards of northern New Mexico had perished. He had no idea what had happened to the soldiers he had sent south to meet the triennial supply train led by Fray Francisco de Ayeta, if indeed the energetic Ayeta was with the supply train (wherever it might have gotten to).

Fray Francisco de Ayeta and Otermín's soldiers, led by Pedro de Leiva, were stalled in El Paso del Norte by the high water of the Rio Grande. Until

August 25, when a messenger from Garcia reached them, they had no hard information that there was any trouble to the north. Then, still unaware of Otermín's plight, Ayeta dispatched Pedro de Leiva with twenty-seven men and supplies for Garcia's refugees.

The first real break in this tangle of confusion and ignorance came when Lieutenant Governor García backtracked to Alamillo to meet with Otermín, who promptly put him under arrest. The charge was that García had abandoned his jurisdiction and set out to leave the province with his soldiers *without* having obtained authority to do so from Otermín. For this transgression, the rules said he had to be imprisoned. García had brought copies of his letters and other communications, which showed he had tried to reach the Governor in the early days of the revolt without success, along with other proof that he was a loyal and effective servant of the King. Otermín insisted on reading all the letters before assuring Garcia that he would be released and absolved of all blame. Even in the midst of a humiliating retreat, with two thousand or more people dispossessed and hungry, with two hundred miles to go before they reached what was now the most northern outpost of Spanish civilization, the formalities of Spanish bureaucratic regulations had to be acted out. It can be little wonder that the entire Spanish empire was creaking and groaning toward its final demise, which would occur a long and expensive one hundred and forty years off into the future.

On the next day, September 6, Pedro de Leiva arrived with twenty soldiers and was overjoyed to see Otermín and the people he had led south from Santa Fe. As Charles Hackett reported, "there were not three of the men Leiva had brought with him to the pass [El Paso] who had not lost, as they then supposed, either father, mother, or children, while all had cause for grief in the loss of more distant relatives and friends."[36] Nonetheless, the meeting of Otermín, García, and finally Leiva at Alamillo made September 6 a day of rejoicing.

Recognizing that the entire group from the north was too low on provisions to go much farther without being resupplied, and realizing as well that the rest of the trek was through harsh desert lands that were frequented by potentially hostile Indians (Apaches and others), Otermín sent a company of soldiers south to El Paso to lead the supply wagons to the pueblo at Socorro where they could all meet up.

## Combined Retreat

Meanwhile Otermín received a letter from San Cristobal by one of the friars who had trekked south with García. He reported that the Rio Abajo people were in dire straits after marching all the way south from Isleta. A bit peremptorily, the friar suggested that Otermín see to it that some provisions be supplied to them or that they be allowed to continue south to El Paso immediately.

Given the sorry condition of Otermín's refugees, he was not just a little put out by what seemed the friar's impertinence. He wrote to the friar of the tribulations he and his group had experienced, and said, "Finally I have come from the pueblo of La Isleta to this place (straining every nerve, as they say) to overtake the people of this camp so that, all being united in one body," they could determine their best course of action in relative safety.

The friar took Otermín's advice and both camps were soon joined at Fray Cristobal, from which they proceeded south, arriving at a place called La Salineta, about ten miles north of El Paso, on September 18. There, on the east side of the still swollen Rio Grande, they saw Fray Ayeta and some twenty-four carts, with attendant mules and drovers—on the west side of the river. Ayeta decided to brave the crossing, diving into the rushing waters along with six spans of mules attached to the first wagon of the train and a number of expert Indian swimmers.

They immediately found that the water was deeper and more treacherous than they had thought. The torrent shoved the wagon completely under water. The mules managed to scramble onto slightly higher ground, but this left the wagon still in the deep rushing water. Ayeta cut the mules loose from the wagon, at which point some of Otermín's men leapt into the water and carried Ayeta to safety—on the east bank of the river.

That night some of Ayeta's men swam their horses through the river with some provisions for the hungry souls on the east bank, and the

*Mother María de Jesús*

following day more wagons appeared, bearing corn, hardtack, flour, sugar, and chocolate, which was passed out to the refugees of both camps. By September 22, Otermín had inspected El Paso, and the monastery of Guadalupe there had accounted for all the food handed out, and had sent men south to procure yet more provisions.

No further record was made until September 29, when every last refugee had reached La Salineta. Otermín ordered a general review of the camp. In all, two thousand five hundred Spanish and loyal Indians had reached the end of the trek. By then, Otermín and the others calculated that four hundred and one soldiers and settlers had been murdered along with twenty-one religious. And that day, September 29, 1680, amassed on New Spain's side of the great river, the Spaniards had for all intents and purposes abandoned New Mexico.

# CHAPTER 14

# The Center
# Does Not Hold

THE AMERICAN REVOLUTION gave the fledgling United States their George Washington. The Revolution of 1789 gave the French their Robespierre and the Terror. The Russians wound up with Stalin. The Pueblos had Po'pay, a man who apparently masterminded the most successful insurgency ever before or after by Native Americans against European occupation, forcing the Spaniards out of their territory and back to what they called New Spain. Po'pay, as noted, was the sort of person who would murder his son-in-law to achieve his goal. What kind of a leader would he be after the revolution?

For one thing, he seems to have altered what might be construed as one of his campaign promises—the one about a wife for every Spaniard you killed. Instead he proclaimed that Pueblo men who had been married to a single wife by means of Christian ritual were to get rid of that wife and marry whomever and however many they chose.

Po'pay was, among other things, a nativist. He pronounced every speck and iota of Spanish works to be offensive and corrupt, and told the Pueblo people they needed to destroy every Spanish vestige. They needed to wash themselves in the running waters of the rivers, and to wash their clothes as well, in order to eliminate any spiritual toxicity of baptismal water and holy oils. No one was to use the names the Spanish friars had given them, or ever to mention again Mary or Jesus or the saints—under pain of a whipping or even death.

In other words, Po'pay called for a complete and draconian housecleaning, a rigorous return to the way things had been before the Spanish arrived in their midst. (Indians who defected to the Spanish in El Paso, or who were captured during brief forays into New Mexico kept the Spaniards up to date to a minimal degree with events among the pueblos.)

Yet even amid the jubilation and fine fury of triumph, not everything the

Spanish had brought seemed evil or something that could not be comfortably accommodated into the aboriginal pueblo cultures. Metal knives, for example. Peaches, for another. And chile peppers. It is not likely that most Pueblo people were avid to go back to a diet of only corn, beans, and squash. So tensions were present from the very beginning of pueblo liberation, just as tensions had been built into the Spanish forms of governance.

The Pueblos seemed to take considerable delight in further defacing and destroying the mission churches and the Spanish buildings. They made certain to burn the casas reales in Santa Fe, and with them all the archives of the Spanish bureaucracy, leaving future historians to prowl around the dusty vaults of archives in Mexico and Madrid for scraps and copies of the elaborate documentation on which Spanish bureaucrats spent their lives.

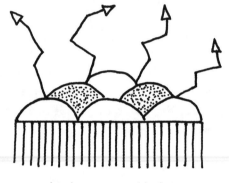

*Clouds, rain, and lightning*

Torching a church made mostly of adobe bricks would seem an unlikely means of destruction. John Kessell has described the way the Pecos people may have turned the soaring mission church, at the time probably the most monumental structure in North America, to rubble.

To begin with, they built a towering pile of dry piñon and juniper branches inside the church, and set it on fire. The flames reached the wooden beams of the roof, and they caught fire, producing a huge draft like "a giant furnace." After the fire died down, the buttressed adobe walls were charred but still standing. Indians climbed over the remaining structure, throwing adobe bricks down by the thousands. Without the support of the side walls, the front wall toppled outward, falling to the ground in a huge, satisfying roar, producing an enormous pile of dried mud rubble, which, with the passage of time and the occasional intervention of rains, would largely vanish back into the earth from whence it came.

Later, the people from Pecos told Spanish interlocutors that they had not destroyed the grand church; it had been the Tewas who had accompanied Po'pay on his triumphal tour of the pueblos. Whoever it may have been, the Pecos people subsequently excavated a large circular kiva, faced with adobes from the church. The "symbolism was clear. The ancient ones had overcome. The saints, mere pieces of wood, were dead."[37]

No one knows how widespread Po'pay's tour was throughout the pueblo world. It is not at all likely, for instance, that he went as far west as Zuni and Hopi. But his grand procession, in which he was accompanied by many of the revolt's leaders, was an occasion to promulgate the new rules, all designed to put an end to the stink of things Spanish. At Santa Ana, Po'pay and the other leaders reportedly threw themselves a bit of a banquet and, seated around a great table, mocked the elaborate courtesies of a Spanish meal. Po'pay

> caused to be brought two chalices, one for himself and one for the said Alonso [Catiti], and both began to drink toasts in scoff at the Spaniards and the Christian religion. And Po'pay, taking his chalice, said to Alonso (as if he were the Father Custodian): "To your Paternal Reverence's health." Alonso took his chalice and rising said to Po'pay: "here's to your Lordship's health, Sir Governor."[38]

Rumors had it that Po'pay was enjoying some Spanish perks, such as Spanish food, while preaching abstinence from all things Spanish. One can wonder if the entire banquet took place, since it seems a bit uncharacteristic of the apparently dour and humorless Po'pay. A captive Pueblo or a defector might well have made the story of Po'pay's hypocrisy up to please the Spanish. In any event, not long after his triumph, Po'pay was forced to step down as the leader of the Pueblo people. We have no idea what events led to his being deposed or if he simply quit.

His place was taken by Tupatu, a milder celebrant of nativist principles from Picuris, but because there was no pueblo tradition of a single leader of all, most, or even some of the pueblos, he was ineffective. In short order, individual pueblos' traditional leaders—religious and secular chiefs—reasserted their proper roles. Pueblos joined (however minimally) with others of their language group, and went their own ways. Before long, the centrifugal forces that had presided over pueblo life probably from their very beginnings thousands of years earlier, returned. Jemez, for example, soon was at war with the Keresan pueblos—Zia and Santa Ana—that were downriver along the Jemez River. Po'pay's single overarching deity, Poseyemu, also was heard from less and less as the pueblos all returned to their own version of the ancients.

## Pueblo Restoration

The first step in reestablishing pueblo life was deciding where to live. Many of the southern and most of the eastern pueblos had already been abandoned, and their inhabitants sought refuge in every place from the Tewa pueblos to the land of the Hopis. Much of the movement was on account of a fear—a perfectly rational one—that the Spaniards, having suffered a terrible humiliation, would eventually build up their forces and return. Therefore, it behooved some of the pueblos to move to more defensible places, which typically meant heading for higher ground.

The Hopis, the farthest from any likely Spanish influence, were happy to tear down the churches—but also happy to hang on to such Spanish benefits as sheep, metal tools, peach trees, and so forth. They moved the site of the first settlement of Hopi clans a half-millennium earlier, the village of Shongopavi, from its natural spring and up onto the point of a mesa high above from which they could see much of the horizon and observe anyone approaching across the painted desert.

Similarly, the Zunis for the first time moved everyone from the six villages to one place, up on nearby Corn Mountain, their slightly less vertiginous version of the great Acoma redoubt. This must have been a grievous inconvenience, since water had to be hauled three hundred feet up on narrow and precipitous trails. Tending the fields below entailed an arduous trip down the mesa's side and back up more or less daily. And of course, housing had to be built.

Archaeologists have since plumbed the old settlements up on Corn Mountain and found several different patterns of home building. The several variations on the traditional Zuni infrastructure were first and foremost a defensive scheme, which is evidenced by the walls built on the edges of the mesa wherever a trail reached the top. Archaeologists have also found rock piles in such places, evidently ammo dumps for discouraging invaders. The Zunis went all out in building living space for the 2,500 or so members of the tribe, in all some thirty-eight structures over an area of more than a hundred acres. Two of these were large room blocks, containing 123 and 148 rooms. In addition, they built ten buildings, each with up to thirty rooms, and another twenty-six buildings of up to ten rooms each. This averages out to about four and a half people per room built on the top of Corn Mountain, which is more than twice what archaeologists think is normal for southwestern pueblos.

## New Lifestyles

The strain of living in tight quarters and in larger groups must have been considerable, calling for new modes of tolerance and new courtesies. The variety of buildings suggests that the prior members of six different Zuni villages were experimenting with many kinds of social space and social relations, in order to permit (or produce) a coherent single tribe. The experiments seem to have been successful. Once they returned to the desert below, twelve years after the actual rebellion, the Zunis all joined in one large village called Halona:wa, on the banks of the Zuni River and now known as the Zuni Pueblo.

One other notable change occurred at Zuni during this period. Before the rebellion, Zuni kivas were separate buildings from the room blocks, and underground. No such places were built on Corn Mountain, but it is, as archaeologist T. J. Ferguson says, "unthinkable" that the Zunis would not have continued their ritual practices on top. It is probable that on Corn Mountain they used interior rooms as kivas, as well as a few open places. Once they moved to Halona:wa, their kivas were located within room blocks too.

Pueblos elsewhere along the Rio Grande moved to high ground. San Ildefonso, one of the major conspirators among the Tewa pueblos, retreated to the high land of Black Mesa. Similarly, San Felipe pueblo, along with Santo Domingo and Cochiti, moved to Horn Mesa where they were joined by some people from Taos and Picuris.

## Shifting Populations

In addition, this period saw a host of what might be called mini-diasporas, impelled by the fear of a Spanish reoccupation. Most of the members of the Sandia pueblo abandoned their traditional lands along the Rio Grande and relocated to Hopi, where they remained into the 18th century, most of them returning to their ancestral lands along the Rio Grande. A group of Tewas camped out below the mesas, hoping for permission to move in. The very remoteness of the Hopi mesas attracted others as well. The Sandias, after what may have been a period of years on the desert below, were refused and returned to their abandoned pueblo on the Rio Grande. On the other hand, a group of Tewas were able to persuade the Hopis that they were superior warriors and would happily take up residence in the eastern side of Hopi as an early line of defense for invaders from the east. They were granted permanent asylum, and today inhabit one of three villages on the top of what is called First Mesa, the easternmost of the three Hopi mesas.

It bespeaks the Hopi sense of themselves and their traditions that most Hopis still consider these Tewa newcomers as hardly really Hopi, even though they have intermarried to some extent and adopted much of the Hopi worldview and ceremonial round. It was a Tewa woman, Nampeyo, who near the turn of the twentieth century invented from old pottery shards the current Hopi style of pottery. Her great-great-grandson, Dan Namingha, is perhaps the most accomplished and famous living Hopi fine artist but is still considered a Hopi-Tewa after merely three centuries of cultural assimilation.

In addition to the movement of large groups, this was a time when individuals or small families took up residence in other parts of the pueblo world. For example, up on Corn Mountain among the Zunis were a handful of Tanos and one Tewa couple, while at the same time, Hopis turned up in pueblos to the east, though not in great numbers. Hopis influenced the renewal of a number of traditions at Isleta and at a new pueblo called Laguna, when it was formed at this time as a kind of adjunct to Acoma. People from Jemez and other pueblos lived among the Navajos, who had managed to avoid much contamination by Spaniards.

Moving, it has been pointed out, has always been a feature of life of the people who became the Pueblos. Their former residences, now ruins, can be found throughout the American Southwest from the Pecos River to the Hopi mesas, from the valleys and cliffs of southern Colorado to Casa Grande in Mexico. Each group, each clan, knows of its ruins, knows their real names, and recalls their time there. Once the last years of Pueblo rebelliousness came to an end, the pueblos were established or reestablished in their current positions on the land. They are now hemmed in by the properties of other people, other organizations including, prominently, the United States government. This is most likely the only time that all the Pueblo people have stayed put for such a long time—three centuries. In a sense then, the Spanish presence can still be felt, not just in the mission churches that have been rebuilt in most of the pueblos but simply where the pueblos themselves are located today.

They can move no more.

PART THREE

# THE PROVINCE REGAINED

# CHAPTER 15

# *The El Paso Connection*

ON SEPTEMBER 29, 1680, Governor Antonio de Otermín ordered that all the bedraggled souls whom he had led south to La Salineta pass muster, reporting on their arms, horses, and other matériel useful for the royal service. One of the things Otermín learned from this muster was that of the 1,946 people present (including servants and Pueblos) only one hundred and fifty-five were capable of bearing arms and fewer than that actually possessed any. The muster also showed the extent of the material losses the Spanish had suffered in the rebellion in addition to the loss of human life. For example, one of the better-off refugees was the ever-loyal Juan Domínguez de Mendoza, whose ambition still was to be New Mexico's governor. According to Hackett, Domínguez

> married, passed muster with a full complement of arms and four additional firearms; a son capable of serving His Majesty, and another younger one; a little girl; thirty-two lean horses and eight mules; three orphan Spanish girls whom he was rearing in his house; and thirty-three servants, young and old. He was robbed by the enemy; and he signs it.[39]

Pedro de Leiva, who had been sent south to help bring the triennial pack train north, did not make out as well as Domínguez. Leiva

> passed muster for himself and three of his sons, all of whom are serving His Majesty ... The enemy killed the wife, two grown daughters, and two soldier-sons of the above-named, three grandchildren and a daughter-in-law being in the pueblo of Galisteo; and of thirty servants whom he had, the enemy left him three, robbing him and his sons of all their property. He signed it.

Far more typical, however, were the fates of such as the four below.

> Pedro de Cuéllar passed muster with four lean horses, an harquebus belonging to his Majesty, and horse-armor of his own, and a boy who serves him. During the rebellion the enemy killed his wife and daughter and robbed him of his few goods. He signed it.

> Sargento Mayor Diego del Castillo, more than eighty years of age, passed muster on foot and without any arms. He is married, with two grown daughters, and all of them are extremely poor. He signed it.

> Miguel Morán, mestizo, passed muster on foot, naked, without arms, and with seven—correction, nine—persons in his family. He did not sign because of not knowing how.

> Catalina de Zamora passed muster with four grown nieces, Spaniards, all on foot and extremely poor, and five servants. The enemy killed two of her nephews and more than thirty relatives. She does not sign because of not knowing how.

From this destitute and grieving group, Otermín was determined to produce a military force that could retake the province of New Mexico. But first he had to arrange for new settlements, however temporary he hoped they would be. He settled the Spanish and their servants southwest of the river where the present-day city of Juarez lies.

Farther south he established three new pueblos with old names—Senecú, Socorro, and Isleta—for the various Pueblos—Piros, Tompiros, Isletans and a handful of others. None of these settlements was well-provisioned nor hopeful harbors in the aftermath of the awful fate these people had suffered. Even though it was considered treason to leave the settlements, the population began to diminish right from the start, people slinking off to seek a better life to the south in the somewhat more civilized lands of northern New Spain.

## El Paso Rebellion

More than a year passed while Otermín sought to organize these pathetic survivors into functioning societies and into an armed force. Meanwhile, news of the pueblo revolt had traveled south and many of the tribes in the region of El

Paso del Norte were dangerously restive and troublesome, hoping to produce their own wars of liberation. Before Otermín could lead a troop north to reclaim New Mexico, he needed to assist in putting down the local upstarts, which he did with the familiar application of lethal force. Finally, in November 1681, Otermín led a column of 146 soldiers, 112 Native auxiliaries, and 28 servants (some of them armed) across the Jornada del Muerte and up the Rio Grande toward Isleta.

*Franciscan*

The faithful Juan Domínguez de Mendoza was one of the Spanish captains among Otermín's force, but many others had declined to join the expedition, doubting any possibility of success. Otermín's hope was that the Pueblos and Apaches would be at war with each other and that the Pueblos, if treated well with pardons for their misbehavior, would welcome the Spanish back in their midst. Otermín was, of course, desperate to retrieve his honor, having lost it with the loss of New Mexico.

Once in Isleta, the Spanish captured about five hundred people, who were promptly absolved by Fray Francisco de Ayeta. Meanwhile, Domínguez led sixty men north as far as Cochiti pueblo. Along the way, most of the Pueblos fled with their livestock, leaving pueblos abandoned except for the old and sick. But at Cochiti, Domínguez and a Captain Pedro Márquez parleyed with Marquez's half-brother Alonso Catiti and other pueblo war leaders. Peace seemed possible.

Otermín marched north on December 11, and set up camp in the Tewa region, near Santa Clara. But a week later, Domínguez heard of a plot to attack the Spaniards and joined Otermín. The attack, they heard later, was to be led by Luis Tupatu of Picuris, who was billed as the commander of the pueblo forces. Otermín decided to abort his frail mission and began his retreat to El Paso, stopping in Isleta and in what seems like a fit of pique destroyed the pueblo's ceremonial sacred objects and burned the place down. On January 1, 1682, with almost four hundred Isletans, and with the agreement of Fray Francisco de Ayeta that such a retreat was well advised, Otermín headed south.

## Reconquest Plans

In the fall of 1683, Otermín was replaced by a new governor, Domingo Jironza Pétriz de Cruzate, who soon moved the new pueblos with old names nearer to El Paso so that they could be put under tighter control. (Earlier, the relocated

Piros had tried to assassinate their priest.) By the end of 1684, the unrest among the Indians south of El Paso seemed to have come under control. But even with this small success, one would imagine that the Viceroy and the King of Spain might have cried, "Enough!" What profit was there in reconquering the pestiferous hordes in New Mexico, that godforsaken province of death and despair? Had the royal treasury not generously financed nearly eight decades of succor and teaching, only to have it wiped away in an instant?

But the forces of the larger world called for reconquest. Soon after the Pueblo Rebellion, the Spanish found that René-Robert Cavalier, Sieur de La Salle, had brazenly traveled south from the French settlements in Canada and claimed the entire Mississippi drainage for the King of France. In eastern Texas, he evidently thought he had easy access to New Mexico, where he would challenge the Spaniards for control. Though LaSalle had neither the equipment nor sufficient troops to succeed in such a venture (and though La Salle was assassinated in 1687), the Spanish decided that reconquering New Mexico was a necessity to provide a buffer zone for the mineral-rich lands to its south. Certainly one might hope for a happier justification for a large province's existence, but being a buffer sounded important at least.

Rather than undertaking the reconquest immediately, however, the Spanish fell to accusing one another of all matter of crimes. In particular, Jironza accused Juan Domínguez de Mendoza (aided by the Santa Fe cabildo) of undercutting his authority in an attempt to grab the governorship of New Mexico. Charges and counter-charges flew, rendering progress impossible, and at the same time the Spanish learned from a few Pueblos who made their way to El Paso that the pueblos were in nearly total disarray.

Jironza headed north to see for himself. In 1689, he found the Zunis and Hopis at each others' throats. The Keresan pueblos, along with Jemez, Pecos, and Taos, were at war with the Tewas and Picuris. The Acomas had split, half of them founding the nearby pueblo of Laguna along with a few disaffected Hopis and some others—the last pueblo to be founded in historical times.

It seems that Jironza, to get even for earlier intransigence, attacked Zia with eighty men and killed what were later claimed to be six hundred Indians, including women and children. Once back in El Paso, Jironza faced another uprising from Indians to his south and, in the meantime, he was replaced as governor of New Mexico by a man who would usher in what many have called a new era in the sad story of New Mexico. This was Diego José de Vargas Zapata Luján Ponce de León y Contreras.

# CHAPTER 16

# Making Peace in Pueblo Country

IN ADDITION TO HAVING A REMARKABLY LONG NAME, Diego José de Vargas Zapata Luján Ponce de León y Contreras was living in New Spain with a few administrative jobs under his belt when in 1688 he was appointed governor of New Mexico. Vargas may or may not have thought this was a career plum, but one did not make a path to glory then as now by turning down a gig.

In 1643, Vargas was born in Madrid into mid-level nobility, meaning he did not have the connections to have a prestigious post or to become a jurist, but he married well and was a devoted husband and father to his family. At age twenty-eight, he left his family behind and took on a governmental assignment in the New World.

His wife died soon after his departure and through his life he wrote lovingly to his children back in Madrid, and kept them up to date with his exploits and finances (which were a bit perilous), always hoping to return to them. He had a second family in New Spain, which, along with his government career, may have kept him on the New World side of the Atlantic.

That he was always, to some degree or another, torn between career and family is to be seen in a fairly typical letter that he wrote to his son-in-law, his lordship Ignacio López de Zarate, from El Paso in September 1691:

Though I am writing to my children, I repeat my blessing to you. May I tell you how comforted I am that they have your lordship's protection and favor. Only with the assurance of their having such a father could I dare to forsake duties so singular in my affection and esteem. . . . Thus, I shall remain in this kingdom in the royal service, as I hope, long enough to see my plans realized.[40]

Only one portrait of Vargas exists. In it he stands in his going-to-the-royal-court finery holding a spear upright in his right hand and an elaborate feathered hat in his left. Leaning slightly to his left and away from the spear as if he didn't like it very much, his body suggests a certain tentativeness. His black hair is long, falling to his shoulders, as was the fashion of his time. He looks directly at the viewer from dark, heavily lidded eyes that are separated by a long, straight nose. His mouth is sensuous and narrow, hardly wider than the bottom of his nose, and surmounted by a narrow mustache. Except for the latter, his soft features and smoothly rounded jaw make him seem boyish, if not feminine. His portrait, in other words, belies the courage and decisiveness with which he undertook the tasks of governor of New Mexico.

The New Mexico appointment was all the less promising, or perhaps more challenging, than it might once have been. For Vargas was named governor of a province the Spaniards no longer inhabited, and which needed to be brought back into the fold. Furthermore, as he soon discovered, what had once been some two thousand disheveled colonists were now a mere five hundred or so, the rest having treasonously slipped away to make new lives somewhere, presumably anywhere but New Mexico. Starting with this tatterdemalion band, Vargas was expected to develop a force that could reconquer the Pueblo Indians and their Apache allies and sometime oppressors, and resume the grand missionary effort of the Franciscans. Vargas accepted the post with grace and even eagerness. He had two quintessentially necessary traits for leadership—vision and self-confidence.

What Vargas found in El Paso on his first visit there in 1691 was not promising—perhaps a hundred male Spaniards capable of bearing arms, three hundred mounts, a presidio (or fort) with only a handful of soldiers, and little food. He wanted to launch the reconquest soon but was called by viceregal authorities to assist in affairs in the province to the south.

Beginning in 1684, the fires of rebellion had again begun to spread throughout lands to the south of El Paso. Oppressed mission Indians rose up against their local friars and civil authorities. The Spanish reacted with violence, putting out one fire after another as they arose. Some historians of Mexico have called it the "Great Northern Revolt," but at the time one Spanish official called it an "epidemic." Many historians suggest that these uprisings among the Indians south of the current U.S. border were triggered by the success of the Pueblo Rebellion, word of which rapidly traveled south.

## Reconquest Begins

Vargas was finally able to proclaim the start of the expedition north to New Mexico on August 10, 1692, twelve years to the day after the Pueblos' uprising. In fact, he left a few days later than that along with fifty soldiers, ten armed colonists, and a hundred or so Pueblo auxiliaries. The Viceroy had promised another fifty soldiers but they arrived after Vargas had managed to get under way. Of course, the expedition included three Franciscans.

To take on what might still amount to sixteen thousand Indians from twenty-five or more remaining pueblos with a force of about a hundred and sixty men would seem more sacrificial than even the charge of the Light Brigade or, closer to home, the defense of the Alamo. Even Otermín had led more than two hundred and fifty men on his unsuccessful attempt in 1681 to regain control of the dismal province. Vargas, however, had information that made his quest seem reasonable, even winnable: chaos among the pueblos. And so he did not intend to use force. Because of his predecessor's account of inter-pueblo strife and current reports from the occasional Pueblo who arrived in El Paso for one reason or another, it seemed possible that diplomacy might serve to return the rebels to the Spanish fold. The Indians would either welcome peace, Vargas believed, or were so divided that they could not offer much by way of resistance. It turned out that both were true.

On the way north past the saw-toothed mountains, the small group of Spanish and Indians saw the ominous smoke of Apache bands on the horizon, but no attack came. Farther on, much of the pueblo world was frozen in an eerie silence; the Tiwa pueblos of Sandia and the others were abandoned. A San Felipe man told Vargas that the Keres Pueblos were glad to welcome him back, especially if he would help them destroy the then hated Tewas, and also the Tanos, who had abandoned their pueblos earlier and now were living in the remaining structures in Santa Fe.

Vargas pressed on to Santa Fe where the Tanos greeted him with scornful jeers and complaints. They shouted out that they wanted nothing more to do with the Spaniards and all the demands they had formerly placed on them. Vargas insisted he had come to pardon them, not to punish them, and made various other offers—for example, that they could retain their own chiefs. The Tanos would have none of it. Meanwhile other Indians, bearing arms, were beginning to arrive from the Tewa pueblos, and Vargas gave the Tanos a two-hour deadline to come out of the villa and be pardoned. The armed Tewas gladly made peace with the Spaniards, and their leader, Domingo, met with the Tanos to persuade them. A few came forth, and Vargas waited patiently until the next day when he entered the villa and pardoned the Tanos; the accompanying friar blessed them and pardoned them in the name of the Church. Vargas repossessed the villa of Santa Fe in the name of Carlos II, the reigning King of Spain.

The following day, Don Luis Tupatu of Picuris arrived with three hundred warriors, taking Vargas up on his promise to consider him a friend in spite of his role in the rebellion twelve years before. The two leaders exchanged gifts and drank chocolate together, and old Tupatu went off, returning the following day with the leaders of several pueblos—mostly Tewa—who saw him as their leader. All these men knelt before the friars and were absolved of any previous wrongs.

As Vargas traveled north through Pueblo country, it was a grand festival of forgiveness and good feelings. People came down from the mesas to reinhabit their pueblos. Children born since 1680 were baptized into the Church, Vargas and the soldiers serving as godfathers. Even the Taos Indians gave in to the peace movement, embracing Tewas, Tanos, and Picuris on whom they had preyed in recent years. The Keres pueblos, promised protection from the same three groups, swore fealty to the Pope and the King—and so too did the Jemez people, though they at first greeted Vargas with hostility and needed extra persuasion. At Pecos, the pueblo's leader inclined to peace with the Spaniards, but many of the younger Pecos people disagreed and left, decamping to elsewhere.

All that was left were the pueblos to the west—Acoma, Zuni, and Hopi—but by now many of the soldiers who had accompanied Vargas north were exhausted, along with their horses. He sent many of them back to El Paso and proceeded west with a mere seventy or so soldiers. They were welcomed at Acoma (after a bit of persuasion) and exuberantly greeted by the Zunis who counted on the Spaniards for protection against Apache raids, which had become more frequent and intense.

From there it was off to the Hopi mesas where the people had been alerted that the Spaniards would act friendly but kill the men and run off with the women and children. At Awatovi, the easternmost Hopi village, the governor, Miguel, welcomed the Spaniards. Vargas performed the repossession rites in the name of Carlos II in Spain and the Holy Father in Rome, and the friars performed various baptisms and absolutions. Even so, some of the Awatovis seemed restive about it all, as did a handful of Utes and Havasupais who were present.

Vargas then set off to "conquer" the other Hopi villages, where he was greeted less than enthusiastically, and decided finally not to go all the way to Oraibi, excusing this oversight by saying that the horses were utterly exhausted. In fact, he had been warned that none of the villages beyond Awatovi were particularly happy at the return of the Spaniards. More than likely, Vargas realized that Oraibi, being the seat of this discontent, was best left alone for the time being.

Vargas returned to Zuni, collected the horses and men he had left there, and returned to El Paso. His accomplishments were remarkable by any standard in Spanish colonial history. In the name of the King of Spain, he had reclaimed twenty-three pueblos and had seen to the baptism of more than two thousand Indians, mostly children. All this had been achieved without any casualties or any outbreak of armed hostilities. His astounding achievement overshadowed the few holdouts. The worst that had happened was the Apache theft of about twenty of his horses.

## Celebrating Spanish Victory

Meanwhile, in Mexico City in the fall of 1692, the Viceroy commanded that the bells of the city ring and the cathedral be illuminated. Much of New Spain was suffering from famine and disease, and food riots had shaken the bureaucracy the previous summer. The opportunity to rejoice for a change and celebrate Diego de Vargas's successful and bloodless reconquest of pueblo country was most welcome. Vargas was cheered as a hero, and the Viceroy proclaimed:

> Many and repeated thanks are his. It is impossible to explain to him the exhilaration and joy he has caused throughout the entire kingdom. He has earned the highest appreciation and esteem of His Excellency and the ministers of the junta, who bear in mind and intend to honor him as a person who by his own deeds proclaims and repeats those of his ancestors.[41]

Vargas himself was rather boastful about his success, saying "I shall remain satisfied, even elated, that no one has been so daring as to undertake what, by divine will, I have achieved thus far."[42] He could surely be forgiven for believing that the conflagration of rebellion in New Mexico had burned itself out. The Pueblo Indians had almost universally sworn obeisance again to the two Majesties and had settled their own internecine squabbles at the behest of their governor. It was the high point in Vargas's professional life.

Vargas then set about planning the second half of his triumphant reconquest

—the recolonization of the pueblo world by Spanish settlers. And while he began to make these plans and to round up willing colonists, the peace he had so skillfully engineered among almost every one of the surviving pueblos had already begun to collapse.

The Viceroy was delighted to provide Vargas with the funds and authority to recolonize and re-missionize New Mexico. Vargas set out on October 4, 1693, with a hundred soldiers, eighteen friars, and about seventy settlers—far fewer than he had hoped for but all that he could scrape up—to accompany him on his mission. With this expedition were also four thousand horses, mules, cattle, and other livestock. The Viceroy promised he would round up more settlers and send them along.

Arriving in the vicinity of Isleta in early November, Vargas was informed that all the pueblos except for Santa Ana, Zia, and San Felipe had changed their minds over the past year, and were opposed to any Spanish incursion. A cause for this reversal, an Indian informer told him, was the work of a man called Tapia who had served Vargas as an interpreter the year before and whom he had left behind among the pueblos. Tapia, it seems, had spent the year explaining that once Vargas returned, he would systematically kill all the Pueblos in retaliation for the uprising in 1680.

After a great deal of deliberation among the Keres people, the half-hearted assistance of old Don Luis Tupatu, and the promised addition to Vargas's expedition of some Pecos warriors, he led his troops to the vicinity of Santa Fe, where Tewas and Tanos had been living since 1680. They were dead set against leaving, but Vargas had determined they must go back to their own pueblos. He and his soldiers invoked the aid of the New Mexico version of the Virgin Mary, a wooden statue called *Nuestra Señora de la Conquista*, which had been spirited out in 1680 and which Vargas, with his usual flair, had thought to bring back. (She is familiarly known today as *La Conquistadora* and is venerated by the Hispanic population in Santa Fe where she resides, though not so much by the Pueblo Indians.)

Rather than split up his forces or leave the colonists in an unprotected camp, Vargas brought his entire colony to the neighborhood of Santa Fe, arriving in deep snow on December 16 and camping a little way off near the mountains. The Spanish were greeted sullenly but quietly by the Tanos and Tewas. While Vargas waited for them to change their minds, the cold, snow, and lack of provisions began to take their toll on the women and children. Reportedly, twenty-two children died and were buried in the snow. The colonists (which included a reconstituted cabildo) did not share Vargas's patience. They met formally with him to demand that they be promptly reinstalled in the houses of Santa Fe.

Vargas waited, but the inevitable battle for Santa Fe began on the morning of December 29. The day before, a Spanish squad had approached the villa to be greeted by what historian J. Manuel Espinosa calls, "blood-curdling shouts interspersed with repellant blasphemy and accompanied by a barrage of stones and other missiles."[43] The next morning Vargas and his troops approached the villa, invoking the name of Santiago, and the battle was on in earnest—continuing through the day and the night.

By the next morning, the Spaniards had won Santa Fe and raised the royal banner over the walls, placing a cross over the main entrance. Many of the Tanos and Tewas fled. Vargas ordered that seventy of the hostiles be executed. Four hundred (including women and children, the number conceivably being a bit of an exaggeration) who surrendered voluntarily were given to the Spaniards and obliged to ten years of servitude.

## Another Revolt

To the Indians, it seemed that Tapia had been mostly right. All of the pueblos except for San Felipe, Zia, Santa Ana, and some members of Pecos resumed a sullen hostility to the Spaniards. People left pueblos to move into the mountains. Rumors of plots against the Spaniards spread like snow over the summits of the peaks. Vargas visited some of the refugees in the mountains and tried to persuade them yet again to sign up with the Pope and the King, but to no avail. Pueblos began raiding the Spanish for livestock and food. The world was again in turmoil and the Apaches gladly did their part in stirring things up, raiding both Pueblos and Spaniards. As spring came, it looked like a starving time ahead, and the Pueblos were at each others' throats.

Vargas found himself in the complex position of needing to attack and raid the food stores of various hostile pueblos in order to feed those pueblos friendly to him. A great deal of bloodshed ensued, with Apaches and then Utes joining in. By the end of 1694, however, the turmoil had been gradually replaced with more peaceful gestures, perhaps out of exhaustion. The leaders of the previously anti-Spanish Tanos and Tewas, for example, were Vargas's guests at Christmas time. The friars had fanned out into the pueblos, were rebuilding the missions, and were now busy with instruction and worship. Many Pueblos helped in the mission fields and supported the friars with gifts of food. All seemed well and at peace again. The Pueblos went to church and also to the kiva, able to practice both faiths without any evident inner conflict.

But the friars still resented the "devil worship" of the Pueblos, and tried their best—once again—to root out all pagan ceremonial and marital practices. To little avail, some of the Pueblos tried to explain to the Franciscans that the repression of native ceremonies was the main reason the Indians had revolted in 1680. But for the most part, the Franciscans continued to act the way they believed Franciscans should act, stamping out paganism, and resentments on both sides simmered.

As early as July, 1695, some of the friars had heard rumors that an Indian plot was afoot—perhaps a general revolt. They brought these fears to the attention of their leader in New Mexico, the custodian, whose name was also Vargas and who assembled a meeting of the friars to consider whether they should all withdraw to the safety of Santa Fe. The rumors of rebellion died down, perhaps because the plot had been discovered.

Yet in December, the friars began to hear rumors again. Fray Francisco Corbera, the missionary at the Tewa pueblo of San Ildefonso, wrote the custodian that an "uprising will take place sooner or later, and although I know [not] the day for which it has been set, I will not leave my mission if I am not ordered to do so in holy obedience. What I do know is that they will kill me or they will take me with them, as they have promised me; in either case there can be no doubt. What I risk is my life."[44]

Fray Francisco went on to write with a peculiar objectivity and profound modesty that it would be better that the Indians take him rather than a saint, "for the power of the agent shines that much brighter when the instrument through which it works is more inadequate and useless."

They were astonishingly brave men, these friars.

A missionary at Picuris who, unbeknownst to his hosts, understood the language, overheard some Picuris ask a boy there if the friar was sleeping. The boy said no, and asked why they had asked him. They replied that they had come to kill him and told the boy to notify them when the friar was asleep.

Tales like these continued like a rising tide, and the Spaniards, particularly the Franciscans, were growing edgier as the spring of 1696 arrived. The friars' calls to their superiors began to show a sense of contentiousness. On June 4, 1696, Fray Alfonso Jiménez de Cisneros took the unusual action of writing directly to Governor Vargas to report that the entire pueblo of Cochiti had gone up to the mesa, taking all their livestock, and that he, Fray Alfonso, had fled to San Felipe pueblo, adding that "it has been by the grace of God that I was able to escape alive from among so many hungry hounds and hypocrites." He warned Vargas to keep his saddle in close view and his hat on his head.

The second Pueblo rebellion was underway.

# CHAPTER 17

# The Second
# Pueblo Rebellion

ON JUNE 4, 1696, about eleven in the morning in the pueblo of San Diego de los Jemez, the Indians called on Fray Francisco de Jesús to come out to give confession to a sick person. As he went out the door of the convent, the Indians caught him, stabbed him repeatedly, and left his dead body lying by a cross he had erected in the cemetery.

At about eight in the evening, Fray Francisco Corbera and Fray Antonio Moreno, a visitor from Nambe pueblo who had come to San Ildefonso for "spiritual consolation," took refuge in a small room in the convent while the people of San Ildefonso, joined by some Apaches, surrounded the pueblo and set the entire place on fire. While the flames rose up, the two friars suffocated from the smoke.

Three hours later, in the pueblo of San Cristóbal, the Indians took the lives of Fray José Arbizu and also Fray Antonio Carbonel, who was visiting San Cristobel to retrieve some of his belongings.

The second pueblo rebellion erupted with five Franciscans and thirty-eight settlers and soldiers dead. Compared to the first rebellion sixteen years earlier, this was relatively tame. Not all the pueblos participated in 1696, and neither was it so crisply organized as the one led by Po'pay. Just who the leaders of this rebellion were remains unclear. It would drag on sporadically for six months instead of being over in a couple of weeks. And though the Spaniards had not known when the second rebellion would occur, they were not totally surprised when it did.

Vargas could count on the loyalty of only five pueblos: three of the Keres pueblos, San Felipe, Santa Ana, and Zia; one Tewa pueblo, Tesuque; and Pecos, though Pecos was, as usual, split into a loyal faction and a hostile one. Some or all of the other eleven—from Santo Domingo north all the way to Taos—were strongly opposed to the Spanish presence. The three western peoples—Acoma, Zuni, and Hopi—were probably among the rebels. On June 5, Vargas faced a daunting and highly confused situation.

One of his first actions was to ask the custodian to order all of the friars who had not already retreated back to Santa Fe. He told the alcalde mayor at Pecos to bring one hundred Indian soldiers to the villa. He sent military squadrons to all of the other places where settlers had gathered for safety. Scouts and spies were dispatched to collect information on the whereabouts and actions of the rebels. Captured rebels who were interrogated (and later typically executed) provided additional information. The summer dragged on with rumor-filled lulls between military actions. Vargas and his soldiers spent a great deal of time in the saddle, first bringing the rebellious Jemez pueblos under Spanish control.

By late July, the Jemez expedition had succeeded and Vargas learned that a rebel leader, Lucas Naranjo of Cochiti, was in hiding with a large group of warriors in the mountains north of the pueblo. In order to reach what they believed to be Naranjo's stronghold, Vargas and his best troops had to pass through a difficult, narrow canyon. Naranjo's rebel warriors were waiting among the rocks, prepared to ambush the Spaniards. The rebels attacked, but Naranjo was soon shot and killed. A soldier marched into view carrying Naranjo's severed head and with that dispiriting development, the rebel warriors fled the field.

Vargas led his troops back to Santa Fe to celebrate this important victory, which he proclaimed a turning point in the campaign of reconquest. Two of the major centers of revolt were now defeated—Jemez and Naranjo's warriors. Vargas then led some troops to Acoma with the goal of calling them down from their redoubt, but they simply refused to come down and after a few days, Vargas returned to Santa Fe. In September, he launched another campaign to Taos and Picuris.

The leaders of Taos were quick to swear fealty to Spain, but when the Spanish arrived at Picuris, they found the pueblo deserted, the people having fled east onto the prairie. Vargas's troops, along with a number of Indian auxiliaries, pursued the Picuris, catching up with them in late October. Vargas captured about eighty men, women, and children as they attempted to escape. The Picuris leaders fled to where the Cuartelejo Apaches lived in western Kansas and, in a terrible irony, were promptly enslaved by the Apaches. Vargas took his captured Picuris back to Santa Fe, where he distributed them to the soldiers and settlers as hostages until the day the Picuris returned to their pueblo.

## *The Second Peace*

Five rebellious pueblos were now subdued, if not at peace. People began to stream back, including some lesser rebel leaders. The rebellion, which ended more in a whimper than a bang, was over. Many of the rebellious Pueblos had left the region for good, taking their chances in the west among the Hopis or north among the Navajos. There were fewer Pueblo people now, the population depleted down to some thirteen thousand by war, disease, and exposure—and the pueblos had lost a disproportionate number of males. The crucial tasks ahead for the Indians were the basic ones of replanting, rebuilding the missions, replenishing the exhausted supplies, and replenishing the population, all of whom had seen little but trouble for the past nine decades.

One of the unplanned side effects of the depletion of Pueblo ranks was that many pueblo fields went unattended, with the result that colonists could now move in on some of the best and most productive lands. This was part of the success met by this new batch of colonists, a success that made it easier to recruit yet more. Soon enough the Hispanic population would greatly outnumber the Pueblos.

Diego de Vargas had proved himself to be one of the most effective administrators the province of New Mexico had ever seen. He expected to be appointed governor for another term, but a man named Pedro Rodríguez Cubero had already been named to that position and took over in 1697. Acting with the combativeness that usually existed between governors, Cubero managed to arouse the settlers and the cabildo against Vargas and imprisoned him. Meanwhile, Vargas had been given the honorary title of "Pacificator" by the royal court in Spain, but the King did not learn until 1700, three years later, that Vargas was languishing in prison in Santa Fe. He was soon released, exonerated, and returned to office. Cubero fled.

The following spring, Vargas was out in pursuit of a band of raiding Apaches when he was felled by a severe fever. He soldiered on but grew more ill and finally had to be carried to the relatively new Spanish town of Bernalillo, on the Rio Grande

*Awatovi warrior with bow, quiver, and shield*

near Santa Ana pueblo. There he made his confession, asked to be clothed in the manner of a Franciscan, and on April 8, 1704, died and was taken to Santa Fe for burial. He was, perhaps, the only true Spanish hero in New Mexico's first century.

Vargas presided over the province at a pivotal point in its history, and it was never again the same. By rising up in 1680 and again in the 1690s, the Pueblo people changed the larger world of the Southwest and elsewhere in many ways that were far-reaching and unforeseen. No one, for example, could have predicted the events that would occur at Hopi shortly after the last of the Pueblo rebelliousness died down.

# PART FOUR

# AFTERMATH

# CHAPTER 18

# Massacre at Awatovi

ONE OF THE DARKEST and most mysterious chapters in Southwestern Indian history took place at Hopi, and in particular at Awatovi, in 1700. It was a response primarily to the feared reemergence of Catholicism. Most of the Hopis had had enough of the Spaniards and their alien religion. They rejected much of anything Spanish in their lives, with the exception of peach orchards and sheep, though sheep are more often obtained from the Navajos than kept by Hopis. From the Spanish point of view, the Hopis were considered the great apostates, refusing any further dealings with the Franciscans, Catholicism, and Spanish—that is, once the affair at Awatovi was in the past. The standard tale of Awatovi involves multiple murders but has been augmented in recent decades—via oral history accounts and recent archival scholarship—to include accounts of witchcraft, amazing escapes, and even cannibalism.

The Hopi versions of most of the events that follow are based on Hopi oral tradition, particularly as collected by Peter Whitely, noted anthropologist, chronicler of the Hopi past, curator at The American Museum of Natural History, and a dear old friend. His conclusions appear in the chapter "Re-Imagining Awat'ovi" in Robert W. Preucel's *Archaeologies of the Pueblo Revolt*.

First, the standard tale.

The Hopi man called Francisco de Espeleta was an apostate among apostates. He had been adopted as a boy by the friar in Oraibi, Fray José Espeleta, who raised him and taught him to read and write, as well as the catechism and the other rites of the Church. Though Fray José taught the boy as much as he could about the ways of the Spaniards, young Espeleta reacted by rejecting, not embracing, his adopted father, Christianity, and any Spanish influence over the Hopi mesas. Instead, he became a highly visible champion and spokesman for the traditional Hopi lifeways. The Spanish came to think of him as the chief of Oraibi, which he wasn't. It is said that in August, 1680, he was one of the two warrior katsinas who dispatched the priest in Oraibi. (Other stories say it was Badger Clan katsinas who dispatched the priest, not warrior katsinas.)

The leader of a Hopi village was (and is) called *kikmongwi*. He is usually drawn from the Bear Clan (in Awatovi the kikmongwi was typically from the Bow Clan), and his role was that of spiritual leader of the village. All other considerations and tasks were of lesser importance, including the job of dealing with the outside world as spokesman or warrior. The kikmongwi was therefore the ultimate power, but his advisors were supposed to keep the mundane matters of life and politics distant from him lest he become distracted from his holy work.

Francisco clearly was no kikmongwi, but he was no doubt operating with at least the tacit approval of Oraibi's kikmongwi in the spring of 1700 when he encouraged a Hopi delegation headed to Santa Fe to tell the new governor, Pedro Rodríguez Cubero, that he, Espeleta, wanted priests to come and baptize the children.

This surely came as a welcome surprise to Cubero. The Spanish knew that Oraibi was the most recalcitrant village, the most firmly determined to maintain Hopi tradition. To the Spanish, it was probably an intimidating place, grim and xenophobic. Even Governor Vargas, after triumphantly visiting all the other Hopi villages to receive their obeisance to Spanish rule, had passed when it came to visiting Oraibi.

Upon hearing the invitation of this "chief" of Oraibi, the authorities quickly dispatched two missionaries to the Hopi mesas—Fray Juan de Garicochea and Fray Antonio Miranda—who arrived in short order at Awatovi, east of the mesas where the other Hopi villages were located. Though the people of Awatovi had participated in the Pueblo Rebellion twenty years earlier and killed the friars at the Mission of San Bernardo, many of them were still (or newly) friendly to the Christian religion, and welcomed into their midst the two new Franciscans who promptly baptized many children. Via a messenger, the friars announced to "Don" Francisco Espeleta in Oraibi their intention to remain at Hopi and bring the gospel to the other villages.

### Violence at Awatovi

But Espeleta was playing a bizarre form of politics—essentially, the game of what one hand giveth, the other taketh away, a tactic to keep his adversaries off-balance. Having invited the Spanish back to Hopi, he soon arrived in Awatovi with what are said to have been eight hundred Hopi warriors armed with bows and arrows. (Eight hundred warriors may be an exaggeration.) No arrows were fired at the appalled and surprised friars, but they received a few whacks from Hopi bows. Under what must have been alarming circumstances, the friars dutifully preached to Espeleta and those among his warriors who understood Spanish—but to no avail. The Hopis remained obstinately hostile.

Two versions exist of what happened next: a Franciscan account says the Hopis returned to their villages, and the friars remained at Awatovi for a few more days, tending to their new converts before heading back to Santa Fe. The Hopi version holds that Espeleta told the friars to leave at once, which they did, with Espeleta suggesting that they might be welcome back at some future point.

In any event, the Franciscans left. Even so, in Awatovi, a large number of people were looking forward to the return of the missionaries and this did not sit well with the village's kikmongwi, a man named Ta'palo, who was disgusted that so many people of his village were untrue to the Hopi way. He concluded that no avenue existed by which he could recreate harmony among his people. Worse, he believed that those who favored the Spanish were "two-hearts," that is to say, witches. He saw the need for drastic action and, to accomplish it, he needed the help of the other village leaders.

Hopis and many other Native people pay a great deal more attention than most non-Native Americans to the meanings and lessons of their past. Only from understanding the past and its lessons, they believe, can one confront modern situations and make proper and informed decisions about the future. The time of their emergence into this world, their fourth, remains a crucial part of their lives.

Sadly, when the Hopis emerged here, a two-heart from the previous world managed to come along unnoticed, resulting in the introduction of evil into this world that they had hoped would be free of it. In the course of their subsequent migrations, they tarried for various periods of time in (and then abandoned) other villages with names like Palatkwapi and Sikyatki, now known only as ruins here and there around the Southwest.

In some of these villages, the two-hearts would become influential, and people would commit a variety of sins—everything from allowing ceremonies to become too elaborate and self-serving, to people ignoring their sworn traditional duties to one another, to the more typical sins of the flesh such as rampant adultery or excessive gambling.

In such instances, the kikmongwi would have to take some drastic cleansing action, such as calling in the Plumed Serpent (a gigantic reptile with definite prehistoric connections to the Aztecs) to flood and destroy the village and the people in it. A righteous and humble few would survive and go on to start a new village on the long path to Hopiland. These cataclysmic solutions were fairly common in the Hopis' history, but they were never taken lightly. As often as not, the kikmongwi would perish as well.

*Sikyatki butterfly*

In this context, Ta'palo of Awatovi went to the kikmongwis of Oraibi and the other three villages (Shongopavi, Mishongnovi, and Walpi). He smoked with each of them, and sought their support for his plan: the complete destruction of his own village. Such a scheme was the direst of proposals and would be an enormous sacrifice on Ta'palo's part. He and his sons would all most likely die. But the evil that had taken root in Awatovi would be torn out like a poisonous plant yanked from the earth, and the Hopi world would be purified. The kikmongwis consented.

By then it was November, the time of year when the men of Awatovi were engaged in the annual ceremonies of the village's manhood societies and, in particular, the time when young men were initiated into the societies' secrets, which occurred every four years. That meant that most if not all the men of Awatovi would be in the kivas, sleeping there.

One morning before dawn, Espeleta led warriors from Oraibi and the other villages up to the wooden gate the missionaries had built before the village. Ta'palo opened the gate, letting the warriors through, and they rushed into the village. At each kiva they pulled up the ladder that led up from below, trapping the men inside. Some shot arrows into the kiva while others gathered firewood from around the village, set it on fire, and threw it down into the kivas along with armfuls of the Spanish red peppers that the Awatovis were particularly fond of. The men below were suffocated by the burning acrid smoke from the hot peppers and seared by the flames. The roofs collapsed on them, sending explosions of sparks and the screams of dying men into the predawn dark.

The warriors swept through the village, herding the thunderstruck women and children out of town, and led them to the other villages where they were to be parceled out as added family members for the warriors.

Some accounts say that all the men of Awatovi perished in the attack;

others say most of the men. But some members of the Hopi Eagle Clan today say that a good number of Awatovis managed to escape into the gloom and trek eastward into Navajo country. They descended into Canyon de Chelly where they farmed along the river that runs through it, planted peach orchards (that are still there), and eventually were accepted as a clan by the Navajos.

Later on the day of the massacre, upon their way home, the warriors and their captives evidently paused at a place called Maschomo (or Skeleton Mound). One version of what happened next is that an argument broke out between the Oraibi warriors and the others over the disposition of the women and children who were to be distributed among the remaining villages. A ferocious fight erupted, leaving a number of warriors and Awatovi women dead. They were buried there, hence the name Skeleton Mound.

The warriors, by the way, did not destroy the village of Awatovi itself. Instead it was simply abandoned, and the passage of time and the forces of erosion turned it into a ruin, its homes and its kivas, some with their magnificent murals miraculously intact, filled with sand. Few Hopis ever went there again; even today few have any interest in walking those ruins, long since excavated by archaeologists but not restored. Few Hopis have any interest in even talking about the massacre at Awatovi, and for reasons not hard to understand.

## Ghastly Findings

In the early 1960s, the story of Awatovi took on a grimmer cast, thanks to an osteologist (or bone specialist) at the University of Arizona, Christy Turner, and his associate, Nancy T. Morris. They made a detailed examination of the remains that had earlier been found and excavated at Skeleton Mound. The early excavators thought that the remains were from a period earlier than 1700 and had nothing to do with what some archaeologists called the "legend" of Awatovi. What Turner and Morris reported was ghastly indeed—the remains of some thirty individuals of both sexes and all ages. Their bodies had been dismembered, burned, cut, and broken. Skulls were bashed in and faces violently smashed. Mutilation was rampant.

Turner and Morris suggested that these were people taken from Awatovi and for some unknowable reason murdered . . . and then eaten.

Turner called this the most convincing evidence of cannibalism in Southwest history. He went on to find, in museum collections, numerous other examples of cannibalism earlier in the archaeological record, suggesting that it was quite common among the Ancestral Puebloan, the people who had built the great monumental buildings at Chaco Canyon, Mesa Verde, and elsewhere and from whom the Hopis are descended. Turner's thesis was not received warmly by the Hopis, especially over his "finds" at Skeleton Mound.

Many archaeologists questioned Turner's estimate that cannibalism was widespread in Ancestral Puebloan times, possibly the result of an influx of Mexican gangs bent on terrorizing the Ancestral Puebloan people in Colorado and New Mexico. Today most Southwestern archaeologists admit that there was some cannibalism, particularly during times of terrible drought. Skeleton Mound remains the only widely accepted instance of cannibalism among Southwestern tribes in historic times.

But another explanation of the carnage at Skeleton Mound was put forth recently, one that is more in tune with the known culture of the Hopis and in keeping with what appears to be the actual situation leading up to the massacre at Awatovi. This version came largely from the work of a blind osteologist from Albuquerque, Marcia Ogilvie.

Ogilvie was present one day when Navajo police brought some badly broken- up remains to New Mexico's Office of the Medical Examiner in Albuquerque. The police were certain these remains were the result of a modern witchcraft execution, which typically involves not only death but the complete wreckage of the corpse—dismemberment and breaking up the bones into small components, the purpose being to make sure nothing remains that is sufficient for the now loose and still evil and vindictive spirit to return to.

Witchcraft is common among many of the Native groups of the Southwest, many of whom believe it is inherited. If suspected of witchcraft, entire families from infants to the elderly may be destroyed. In any event, Ogilvie looked at the bones (which she does with her hands, of course) and realized that the Navajo remains were remarkably similar in virtually every feature to Turner's descriptions of the bones of people who have been cannibalized. Perhaps, she suggested officially to her colleagues at scientific meetings, many of the instances of cannibalism as interpreted by Turner are in fact instances of a community ridding itself of witches.

Certainly Ogilvie's suggestion accords more closely to the nature of Hopi society in historical times. There is no suggestion of cannibalism among the Hopis either as a ritual (gaining strength from the dead) or as a matter of nutrition, say, during the periods of frightful extended drought that have from time to time left hundreds of Hopis dead from starvation. (There are provable instances of cannibalism in the Mesa Verde region of southeastern Colorado, where the ancestors of some of the Pueblo people were from, but few careful students of this believe it was as prevalent as Turner has made it out to be.)

Ogilvie's suggestion of a witchcraft killing at Skeleton Mound would explain the smashed-in faces—certainly an act extraneous to food preparation such as extracting the brains, but understandable as a frantic and outraged attempt to render a body no longer inhabitable.

According to Hopi oral history, one of the details that one hears about these events is that Ta'palo, the kikmongwi of Awatovi, was convinced that at least some of his people who favored the return of the Spanish and the friars were witches. That their identities would have been known to some of the warriors from other villages is not a great stretch at all, and that they would have to be dealt with harshly and permanently lest they infect the other villages would not be illogical. Eating them, however, would make no sense at all; they would be highly toxic.

Yet another detail has been adduced to the massacre story, fitting it perhaps more precisely into the fabric of Hopi life and belief, chiefly by Peter Whitely, curator of anthropology at The American Museum of Natural History in New York. His insights are based particularly on the nature of several manhood and women's societies, most of which evidently originated at Awatovi under the leadership of the Bow Clan and a couple of other clans there—Tobacco and Badger.

Membership in one or another of the secret societies raises one to the level of a spiritual adult. One of the manhood societies, called *Wuwtsim*, held (and still holds) its initiation in November, the time of year of the massacre. Ridding the world of the Wuwtsim men who would have been in their kiva must have had something to do with destroying or reducing the power of the Bow Clan and something to do, as well, with Christianity. In any event, it seems that a number of Awatovi people survived the holocaust aside from those who escaped and threw in their lot with the Navajos. A Tobacco clan man from Awatovi is thought to have brought all the sacred paraphernalia for several secret societies to the other villages and introduced those ceremonies to them. There is some evidence that Ta'palo was the Tobacco Clan member himself, who escaped and brought a revised version of the Wuwtsim ceremonials to the other villages along with two other societies' secrets.

Without going into further detail about clan relationships and other often highly arcane matters, all this suggests to Whitely that the Hopis were engaged in a scheme of revitalization of Hopi society and in some sense a purification—in part a way of putting the entire Spanish experience to rest. Added to this is the presence at the time of people from many Rio Grande pueblos, many of them melting into the Hopi culture and population.

In any event, the useful ceremonies of the various secret societies were altered in the process of being transferred from Awatovi to the other villages—in essence, purifying them so that their usefulness to the Hopi could continue to this day.

The ramifications of the Pueblo Rebellions of 1680 and 1696 for the world of the Hopis are probably even more complex than what anyone today really knows or ever will know. The same surely applies to the Zunis and the other Pueblos, all of whose histories are as complex and probably, from time to time, as dark as the Hopis'. The other Pueblos have all been a great deal more private about such things. They look askance at the openness of the Hopis. The Rio Grande Pueblos in particular took to heart the secrecy they had to employ under Spanish rule in the seventeenth century to continue their ceremonial life. They have kept most such private matters private.

# CHAPTER 19

# Causes and Effects

THE PUEBLO REBELLIONS OF 1680 AND 1696 can be considered the first American revolution—fought in large part if not entirely for the right of the Pueblo people to practice their religion and cultural ways without interference. In other words, to live free. Their ancient practices had kept the Pueblos safe, populous, and reasonably prosperous for as long as they had lived along the Rio Grande and its tributaries. The Spanish invasion and occupation was a long story of discomfort for the Indians, punctuated with numerous tragedies. In their attempt to upend the culture of the Pueblo people, the Spanish weakened it but failed to replace it with a means to achieve peace or prosperity. More than likely, Po'pay and the other leaders saw the distinct possibility that the Pueblo people—down to some thirteen thousand from about sixty thousand in the course of eighty years—might well disappear altogether if they did not reconstitute themselves along traditional (tried and true) principles.

Not long after the 1696 rebellion, settlers—mostly Hispanic—outnumbered the Pueblos by a large margin. The Pueblo people would never again rise up in anger and rebel. Those days were over; insurrection was no longer a possibility or a necessity. Given the continuing raids by Apaches, Navajos, and later Comanches as well, the Pueblos and the settlers realized that mutual cooperation was the order of the day. At the same time, with the Hispanic settlers growing in number, the Franciscans' numbers—and activities—were diminished.

The Franciscans never regained their earlier power over the affairs of the province. Indeed, the primary reason for the colony's existence was no longer the conversion of the "heathen Indians" but to serve as a geographic buffer to keep the rival empires of England and France away from the still valuable mining districts to the Pueblos' south. The Franciscans, now of lesser status, soon realized that it was time for them to look the other way when the Pueblos performed the "katsinas" and their other rites.

The missions were rebuilt in most of the pueblos, and the Franciscans continued to say mass. But in the plazas, the katsinas danced in the sun again as well. There arose a mutual accommodation, with Pueblos taking on certain of the Spanish ways. Monogamy came to be the Pueblo norm, for example, as did a Catholic modesty in dress.

Not long after the end of the rebellion in 1696, the Pueblos were able to live with two separate but intertwined traditions of a religious nature. One can see this acted out during the feast days of the pueblos when they celebrate their patron saints or other holidays. In the prosperous Keresan pueblo of Santo Domingo, which lies along the Rio Grande between Albuquerque and Santa Fe, some of the ceremonial life has accommodated itself to the Roman Catholic calendar. The celebrating of Christmas, New Year's Day, and Easter are their most public and accessible ceremonies. After a midnight mass in the mission church, the patron saint (in the form of a carved statue) is carried prayerfully to a shrine in the vast plaza. Public dances follow through the day. These dances consist of hundreds of costumed men, women, girls, and boys—all from the two kiva groups, the Turquoise and the Squash societies—alternating as dancers in the plaza to the accompaniment of a large group of singers and drummers. It is altogether an awesome performance, continuing until the late afternoon sun lights the pueblo gold.

Outside the plaza, in the pueblos' orderly north-south and east-west streets, arrays of vendors from other pueblos sell food, jewelry, pottery, baskets, and, among other items, ice-cold watermelon crush that brings a wondrous relief from the heat and the wind-borne dust. It is a grand festival, and an equally spectacular public Corn Dance is performed annually on August 4.

Santo Domingo is one of the most conservative pueblos. Ethnologists and others have been unable to ferret out much in the way of specifics about the pueblo's private ceremonial and social customs. It is known to be a highly theocratic and structured society, many of whose members carry on professional, managerial, and other jobs in Albuquerque and Santa Fe.

## Repercussions and Impacts

The Pueblos' revolt had repercussions well beyond the Rio Grande valley and the western mesas. To the south in Mexico, as noted earlier, numerous tribes heard of the uprising of 1680 and rebelled, none with the precision of the Pueblos but certainly tying up the Spanish authorities for several years, and postponing de Vargas's return to New Mexico in the 1690s.

Meanwhile, after the Spanish had set themselves up in El Paso, many of the Pueblo people sought other places to dwell, given that the Spanish would surely attempt to return to the Rio Grande valley in due course.

A considerable group of Tewas abandoned their pueblos and went to Hopiland, as did a number of other groups. And when the Spanish did return, a number of Towa-speakers from the Jemez pueblos headed north to live among the Navajos in the San Juan Valley, where they plotted the re-expulsion of the Spaniards. This did not happen, of course, and the Pueblos simply settled in with their Navajo hosts.

Some scholarly disagreement exists, but it seems that the basic Athabaskan worldview of the Navajos underwent a significant change as a result of the influx of Pueblo people. In any case, what follows is what one hears today from some Navajo storytellers.

*Bird design, Pecos pottery*

The Pueblos at Navajoland soon enough intermarried with their hosts, and many pueblo traditions caught on. It has been said that Navajoland (which they call *Dinétah*) became for a time the center of a cultural development unrivalled in any other Athabaskan group. For example, the Navajos typically farmed but also roamed far and wide on hunting (and raiding) expeditions, but now some of them became more sedentary, like the Pueblos. Pottery unearthed from this period shows the distinct polychromatic designs of the Pueblo style—the imaginative geometry of black on white or black on orange. It is presumed that Navajo women made some of this.

In the canyons and tributaries of the San Juan River, single and multi-room buildings became the norm (rather than a few isolated such buildings that predate this period). Katsinas are found dating to this period etched into natural rock surfaces of Dinétah. The pueblo kiva, however, never did catch on; the six-sided *hogan* (pronounced Ho-GAHN) remained the religious structure of choice. Many elements of the pueblo creation stories found a home in the Navajo creation stories, such as the tales of twin brothers in very ancient times clearing the world of monsters and making it safe for people. The Diné (Navajos' name for themselves) emerged into this fourth, glittering world after a long and difficult migration through three earlier ones. Clan membership may or may not have become more important at this time, but various Pueblo taboos, such as the one against eating fish, are known to have been adopted.

Most traditional societies resist change, but not so with the Navajos. They have always been highly adaptive, even opportunistic, and part of this may be explained by their language, which, as anthropologist Gary Witherspoon has pointed out, is dominated by active verbs, reflecting the Navajo view that things "are constantly undergoing processes of transformation . . . and that the essence of life is movement.[45] In any event, Navajo culture diverged from its Athabaskan roots and became something new, perhaps more complicated and beautiful.

Beginning in the mid-1700s, a nativist revitalization of older Navajo traditions and ways took place. A major shamanistic feature called the Blessing Way, a multi-day-and-night ceremony, came into prominence at this time (but it tells of the trail through three worlds into this one). Many Pueblo traits and concepts seem to have been done away with, such as stone houses, decorated pottery, and katsinas. But many pueblo cultural traits remained, transformed but still present. One Navajo clan, for example, the Coyote Clan, has two branches, and the Turquoise branch traces itself directly back matrilineally to the people from Jemez.

We cannot say that Navajo culture would not have changed greatly as the groups of part-time farmers–part-time hunters took on Spanish sheep and the lifeways of the pastoralist. It surely would have. But the influx of Pueblo people as a result of the Pueblo Rebellion surely was part of what the Navajo Nation today—the largest single land-based Indian tribe in the United States—has become. The Blessing Way, including their versions of many Pueblo stories and characters, has been translated into English (as the book *Diné Bahane'*) and many consider it a major, truly Native American epic.

## Coming of the Horse

Beyond such a local, Southwestern influence, the Pueblo Rebellion also altered history in a geographically greater region, the Plains, ushering into being what is generally perceived to be the most romantic era in all of Native American history. It has to do with an animal called *Equus equus*.

In the course of writing this book about the Pueblos and the Spaniards I have from time to time asked myself what would have happened if the Pueblo Rebellions had not occurred until much later—say a century later? The Pueblo

Rebellion of 1780. With that single alternative "fact" as the frame, we need to drop back in time and look at one phenomenon of the Pueblo Rebellion that rarely gets much emphasis.

Horses evolved over a very long period of time in North America, but by the end of the last Ice Age some ten thousand years ago, they had disappeared from this continent, escaping whatever conditions existed by migrating into Asia over the Bering land bridge. They returned only when the Spanish arrived in the early 1500s, bringing small herds of horses on their small ships. Mounted on a horse, a soldier looked pretty invincible and, to people who had never seen such a thing, a mounted horseman looked like an intelligent monster, an armed centaur.

The Spanish used this weapon to their great advantage wherever they went to establish their empire, and they always guarded their horses ruthlessly. Consider the amount of sheer useful energy a horse possesses that becomes a tool of the rider, compared to a two-legged man. The Spanish didn't want any two-footed barbarians learning how to ride (or use a gun) so they tried to keep them strictly to themselves. This was the case in New Mexico in the 1600s.

Occasionally, Apaches and other raiding tribes rode off with untold numbers of Spanish horses, but with the revolt in 1680, the number of stolen horses reached well into the thousands. Soon the Apaches had enough horses to terrorize not only the Pueblos but many of the plains people to their east and north—village-dwelling Pawnees and Otos. The Utes also had stolen some horses from the Pueblos, but it would be several decades before they used them for riding, first putting them to work hauling things on travois, a great improvement over dog-pulled travois.

In 1680, most of the people who lived on the plains lived in villages most of the year, such as the semi-sedentary Mandans and Arikaras along the upper reaches of the Missouri River. And at about this time, some agricultural people who would eventually be called the Cheyenne had started to leave their villages in Minnesota and head west. Beavers had been over-trapped, but bison roamed out on the plains that could be hunted on foot the old way—chasing them over cliffs. By the 1770s, the soon-to-be-called Cheyenne were living in three Mandan-like villages along the upper Missouri River. The French and the British were trad-ing guns to all these northern plains tribes for bison pelts. And in the southern plains, the Apaches were successfully raiding just about everyone.

Not until a few decades later would the Plains Indians find themselves in possession of horses and guns, both astonishingly powerful weapons. Among them were the Cheyenne and their fellow ex-Minnesotans, the Sioux. Thus armed, they became the most potent tribes on the Plains, with one exception.

Some of the Shoshones had pushed their way out of the Rocky Mountains onto the plains, and one branch came to be known as the Comanches. Similarly armed and mounted, the Comanches would become what are probably the greatest light cavalry ever known, pushing the Apaches back to the south and harassing the Pueblos, the Spanish, Texans, and anyone else who got in their way.

This "horsing" of the plains is what created the emblematic American Indians in the minds of most of the world—superbly equestrian, elaborately feathered, warlike, daring to the nth degree, artistic, courageous, given to dying for honor, and fighting the onslaught of encroaching Americans in the form of the United States Cavalry against all the obvious odds and zealously to the death. These were, most notably, the Cheyenne, Sioux, and Comanches, along with others less famous. And these new cultures would be fairly short-lived—dominating the plains for a bit less than a century.

Of course, if the Pueblos had risen up not in 1680 but, say, a hundred years later, it is highly unlikely that horses would have reached the Cheyenne, Sioux, Comanches, and the others for yet another fifty years or so—say 1840. By then the ranchers, railroad workers, gamblers, drifters, prostitutes, sheriffs, school marms, and the U.S. military had already begun to trickle into the plains, the opening guns of relentless American Manifest Destiny. The grand Native horsemen of the buffalo plains probably never would have gotten underway.

In real history, however, horses were loosed onto the Plains in significant numbers in 1680, permitting the horse cultures to arise and to liven things up (to say the least) for about a century during which they reinvented themselves and reigned supreme—the gift, indeed, of Po'pay and the rebellious Pueblos of 1680.

## Importance of the Pueblos

From the beginning of contact with the Rio Grande pueblos and those to the west, Europeans sensed something special about the Pueblos. In 1620, a royal decree established the civil office of governor in each pueblo, a position to be held by a native member. The badge of office was a silver-headed cane. The cane signified the governor's authority and the sovereignty of the pueblo. A cross inscribed in the silver head signified the pueblo's loyalty to the Church. In addition, over the years the Spanish crown awarded the pueblos grants of land of various sizes in the pueblos' surround.

The Spanish did not hand out canes (or land grants) to any other Native American tribes on the continent (except the Tohono O'odham of southern Arizona)—not the Californian tribes once the Spanish began to build a long string of missions up the coast, or any Florida tribes. During the eighteenth century, the Pueblos and the Spanish reached a more or less peaceful *modus vivendi*.

The Spanish did occasionally abuse Indian labor, but the years of the encomienda were over. The Pueblos usually supplied most of the troops to ward off the so-called "wild tribes" or to make retaliatory raids on them.

Many of the Spanish canes have survived to this day, along with two other batches. The second batch was handed out to the Pueblos by the new Republic of Mexico after the Mexicans (along with much of South America in this period) had revolted and ejected Spain in 1821. A third batch of silver-headed canes was sent to the Pueblos by President Abraham Lincoln in 1863, with thanks for Pueblo support of the Union.

The canes from Mexico were accompanied by the announcement that all Indians under the jurisdiction of the Mexican government were citizens. But the Mexican government was even less successful than its predecessor at warding off raids by the Apaches, Navajos, and more recently arrived Comanches.

Nor was the new government assiduous in keeping Hispanics from muscling their way onto Pueblo lands and claiming them for themselves. The Mexicans also opened the door to French and then American adventurer/traders and trappers, the Spanish having always tried to isolate New Mexico from any non-Spanish European influence. Another significant change in this period was the departure of the last of the Franciscans. The missionary project had dwindled over the years, with some of the churches being "secularized," meaning that they were led by secular (diocesan) priests, not members of any religious order. In fact, most of the churches in New Mexico were left unstaffed by any clergy except deacons, who could perform baptisms but could not celebrate mass or hear confessions.

In 1846, only twenty-five years after the Mexican regime began, the President of the United States, James K. Polk, sent American troops against Mexico in a war that would last two years and that brought under the U.S. flag practically all of the American West that was not included in the Louisiana

Purchase or Texas (which had been summarily annexed the year before). What would become the states of California, New Mexico, Arizona, Utah, and Nevada were all gobbled up as part of America's Manifest Destiny—itself one of the most potent land acquisition schemes in all of history. The Treaty of Guadalupe Hidalgo that made all this official let stand many grants awarded by the Spanish crown and later the Republic of Mexico to the Pueblos and the colonists. Not altogether explicit about the actual boundaries of such lands, and sometimes overlapping by one degree or another, the land grants would be a source of argument even into the twenty-first century.

That the Mexican regime in New Mexico was over had become apparent on August 18, 1846, when a seventeen-hundred-man American army, called the Army of the West, led by General Stephen Watts Kearny, arrived in Santa Fe unopposed. This was one of the early maneuvers of the war with Mexico. Kearny was charged with setting up a civil government for New Mexico. In the United States, of which New Mexico was now a territory, Indians were not allowed citizenship, so the Pueblos abruptly became noncitizens again. But the Pueblos were clearly village-dwelling agriculturalists and at least some of them appeared to be devout Catholics as well. So they were not considered Indians (in the sense of wild savages) either. They would remain in an ambiguous position in the minds—and the laws—of the makers of Native American policy well into the twentieth century. What this meant, for example, is that the various national intercourse laws, dating back to pre-Constitution times, that prevented state or local land deals with Native tribes unless a federal officer was present, did not apply to the Pueblos. (The intercourse laws would be invoked in the late twentieth century to give eastern tribes like the Pequots huge financial settlements for lands lost in violation of these laws.)

One of the chief responsibilities of the civil government in New Mexico was the protection of the Pueblo villages from the raiding that persisted at least sporadically between stretches of time when the Pueblos and the "wild tribes" traded peacefully. But by the 1860s, as the Civil War got under way, the U.S. soldiers in the region essentially vanished, and the raiding became more frequent and intense.

## The Long Walk

In 1863, General James Carleton was dispatched to New Mexico with a regiment of California volunteers. He decided to round up as many Navajos and Apaches as possible and intern them in a place called Bosque Redondo and also Fort Sumner. One of the worst events in the long history of the Navajos took place when eighty-five hundred men, women, and children were marched hundreds of miles across New Mexico to what amounted to a concentration camp, to be taught the arts of peace and the truths of Christianity. About 10 percent of the Navajos died on what is known as the "Long Walk" from dysentery, fatigue, exposure, and outright murder. Many more died at Fort Sumner until four years later when even the New Mexicans protested, and the Navajos were sent to a reservation that lay across the current border between New Mexico and Arizona, west of their original lands in the region.

The Long Walk was one of the early instances of the U.S. government policy of rounding up the Native tribes of the West and settling them in reservations usually not in their original lands, and often with tribes that were mutually hostile. These were all, to one extent or another, land-based tribes, their identity tied to their landscape in many important ways. Uprooting them was designed not only to get them out of the way but to hasten the end of their cultural identities, in the hope that they could be turned into peaceful farmers and yeomen. Many of the tribes treated in this manner have indeed lost some if not all their cultural identities.

Such disruption was something that the Pueblos, seen as not really altogether Indians, did not have to suffer, another reason along with the rebellion for their continued cultural cohesion. Hemmed in today by Anglo and Hispanic neighbors, the Pueblos can no longer move, but they do remain on their ancestral lands where most of them have lived for five hundred years or more.

## *Politics and Land Disputes*

Inevitably, both Anglos and Hispanics continued to look covetously at the pueblo lands and the water rights that went along with the lands. They developed various techniques for whittling away at them, including renting grazing land from a pueblo, then paying taxes on it, thus getting their name officially associated with it, clouding the issue of title. The matter would then be adjudicated by judges in Santa Fe who mostly felt little compulsion to side with Pueblo interests. The pueblos continued to be seen simply as individual municipalities, subject to the vagaries of territorial, and then state law once New Mexico became a state in 1912.

Pueblo lands became subject to a full-scale attack in 1922. Albert Fall, the

Secretary of the Interior and a former U.S. Senator from New Mexico (and the creator of the Teapot Dome scandal that would force him from office), persuaded then New Mexico Senator Holm O. Bursum to introduce a bill in the Senate that would "settle" once and for all the land disputes and ambiguous titles involved in pueblo country.

The bill would become known as the Bursum Bill and it gave non-Native claimants title to the land if they could prove possession by June 10, 1910, by one means or another (none of which would stand up to much scrutiny, but scrutiny was not really called for in the bill). If a claimant "proved" possession, the federal government would pay the pueblo involved for the loss of the land in dollars or land, but the bill provided that any lands thus acquired did not bring with them any new rights to water, by which the land could be made productive. The U.S. Senate passed the Bursum Bill on September 11, 1922.

The Pueblos responded by drawing together in monolithic opposition, a unity of purpose not seen among them since 1680. With the help of a young social worker from New York, they issued an appeal to the public press and to other Indian tribes that accused Bursum of a major deception. Bursum had told his Senate colleagues that the Pueblos had requested such a bill. On the contrary, the Pueblos said, they had never asked for such a bill, and if passed it would destroy their way of life and all their traditions. They asked if the American people were willing to see this happen.

Many were not. The Bursum Bill never made it through the House of Representatives and was subsequently dropped altogether. Thus, the Pueblos had learned again the value (and the power) of acting in unison in their common interests. And at about this time, in the 1920s, a new force began to emerge to help the Pueblos' ability to survive: tourism. With trains came tourists eager to see the West and its "exotic" inhabitants. There soon arose a major trade in traditional Pueblo crafts—especially pottery and jewelry and, in the western pueblos, carved fetishes and katsina dolls. This trade helped numerous Pueblo families to enter the cash economy and sustain themselves through the years. These crafts—many now considered fine art—along with the public ceremonies held in many of the pueblos, continue to be a major draw for tourists, whose visits comprise a major part of the state's business. For example, every year in August, thousands of people flock to Santa Fe to attend Indian Market, when the streets of the old provincial capital are lined with hundreds of booths filled by Indian artists with juried invitations to attend. Many of them are Pueblo artists selling jewelry, pottery, and other artworks.

The Indian Pueblo Cultural Center in downtown Albuquerque, representing all the Rio Grande pueblos along with the western ones, acts as an important welcome and introduction to the Pueblo world.

Over the years in the twentieth century, the Pueblos became a considerable political force in New Mexico, more so toward the end of the century, with many of them building casinos on or near their lands. The casinos have been cash cows for those pueblos that have them, and they also have been controversial—among Pueblo people as well as non-Natives. There have been instances of illegality, but most of the pueblo casinos have operated within federal and state law, and have concluded agreements over what portion of the profits should go to the state.

A shining example of exactly the kind of self-sufficiency the pueblos with casinos have sought to create is found in the little pueblo of Sandia, on the northern border of Albuquerque, lying between the Rio Grande and the Sandia mountains to the east. Sandia is home to about four hundred very private people. With the proceeds from gambling, they have built a health center and medical–dental clinic for their people that the Kellogg Foundation cited as a model of rural health care. They built a superior elementary school for themselves and may be the only community in the nation with a policy of zero tolerance for dropping out of school. A scholarship fund ensures that Sandia youths will be financially able to take their education to graduate and advanced degrees. Pueblos (and other tribes around the country) that have profitable casinos and have invested the proceeds wisely have made themselves essentially self-sufficient, no longer needing to depend on federal funds. The Pueblos, as Tewa anthropologist Alfonso Ortiz said, have made themselves a universally welcomed and culturally important part of the fabric of New Mexico, as have the Hopis in Arizona.

## Pueblo Point of View

About three decades ago, in the spring of 1980, my wife Susanne and I visited a man of the San Juan pueblo, Herman Agoyo, in his office in a trailer parked just outside the pueblo where Juan de Oñate established his headquarters in 1598. Agoyo, a soft-spoken and slightly professorial man, was responsible for organizing the tercentennial celebration of the Pueblo Revolt, including a long-distance relay race to be run from Taos through Pueblo country all the way west to the Hopi mesas, an overall distance of more than three hundred miles. Agoyo was and still is an exemplar of the modern era of cooperation among the still multilingual pueblos that began in earnest in the 1920s. He has held numerous positions calling for and encouraging such inter-pueblo cooperation in their common interests.

He explained that had it not been for the Pueblo Revolt, pueblo culture would probably have failed to survive. He pointed to those Pueblo Indians—mostly from Isleta—who joined the Spanish in their retreat from New Mexico, and others who joined them later in what is today called Isleta, Texas. "They have lost their culture, their languages," Agoyo said, adding, "Pretty much all that we up here hold dear."

Such losses are unfortunately very common throughout the United States, where Indian communities have suffered under the steady gale-force pressures of the dominant society and the failures of U.S. federal Native American policies. Some experts have opined that by the year 2050, only some fifty of the original three hundred-plus native languages of North America will still be spoken. Among them, almost certainly, will be the languages of the Rio Grande pueblos and the western pueblos—Acoma, Zuni, and Hopi. For example, thanks to the late Emory Sekaquaptewa of the Hopi Eagle Clan, a linguist at the University of Arizona, a huge dictionary and grammar of the Hopi language now exists—a thirty-thousand-entry tome that facilitates the shift of the Hopi language from oral only to both oral and written. Other pueblos, gaining control over their own schools in the past forty or fifty years, now have the opportunity to teach each new generation how to speak and, in some cases, write their own precious languages with their own profound meanings and unique ways of looking at and understanding the world.

Who knows what the rest of us might learn from them in the years ahead?

# Endnotes

1. Hackett, *Revolt of the Pueblo Indians*, xxxiii.
2. Quoted in Chavez, *My Penitente Land*.
3. Ibid.
4. Elliott, *Spain and Its World*, 72.
5. Personal communication from Emory Sekaquaptewa, Hopi Eagle Clan.
6. Leeming and Page, *The Mythology of Native North America*, 11.
7. Page and Page, *Hopi*, 152ff.
8. Kessell, *Kiva, Cross & Crown*, 108.
9. Ibid., 105.
10. Ibid., 123.
11. Ibid., 129.
12. Kessell, *Kiva, Cross & Crown*, p. 129.
13. Morrow, *Harvest of Reluctant Souls*, 5.
14. Ibid., 4.
15. Ibid., 15.
16. Ibid., 57.
17. Ibid., 37.
18. Minge, *Acoma*, 23.
19. Weber, *Spanish Frontier*, 97.
20. Kessell, *Kiva, Cross & Crown*, 174.
21. Riley, *p.* 161.
22. Weber, *Spanish Frontier*, 130.
23. Gutiérrez, *When Jesus Came*, 126.
24. Bloom and Walter, *New Mexico Historical Review*, 435.
25. Hurtado and Iverson, *Major Problems*, 103.
26. Gutiérrez, *When Jesus Came*, 131.
27. Kessell, *Kiva, Cross & Crown*, 223.
28. Riley, *Kachina and the Cross*, 221.
29. Gutiérrez, *When Jesus Came*, 131.
30. Hackett, *Revolt of the Pueblo Indians*, xlv.
31. Espinosa, *Pueblo Indian Revolt of 1696*, 35.
32. Ibid.
33. Hackett, *Revolt of the Pueblo Indians*, 177.
34. Ibid., 102.
35. Ibid., 61.
36. Ibid., ccix.
37. Kessell, Hendricks, and Dodge, *Letters from the New World*, 239.
38. Lummis, *Land of Sunshine*, 309.
39. Hackett, *Revolt of the Pueblo Indians*, 137–153 has the entire muster list.
40. Kessell, Hendricks, and Dodge, *Letters from the New World*, 118.
41. Ibid., 51.
42. Espinosa, *Pueblo Indian Revolt of 1696*, 53.
43. Ibid., 159.
44. Whitely, *Bacavi*, 19.
45. Witherspoon, "Language and Reality," 570.

# Bibliography

I HAVE PUT AN ASTERISK before the titles of those books listed here that were the most relied upon. Most of the others gave me helpful background information, some only minimally related to the project at hand.

*Allen, Craig D. "Ecological Patterns and Environmental Change in the Bandelier Landscape," craig-allen@usgs.gov.

Baldwin, Louis. *The Intruders Within.* New York: Franklin Watts, 1995.

Barrett, Elinore M. *Conquest and Catastrophe: Changing Rio Grand Settlement Patterns in the Sixteenth and Seventeenth Centuries.* Albuquerque: University of New Mexico Press, 2002.

Blacker, Irwin. *Taos.* New York: Pocket Books, 1959.

Bloom, Lansing, and Paul Alfred Walter. *New Mexico Historical Review,* vol. 12, no. 1, 1937.

*Carlson, Paul H. *The Plains Indians.* College Station, TX: Texas A & M University Press, 1998.

*Chavez, Fray Angelico. *My Penitente Land.* Santa Fe: Museum of New Mexico Press, 1974.

Cordell, Linda S., and George J. Gumerman, eds. *Dynamics of Southwest Prehistory.* Washington, DC: Smithsonian Institution Press, 1989.

*Courlander, Harold. *The Fourth World of the Hopis.* New York: Crown Publishers, 1971.

*Elliott, John Huxtable. *Spain and Its World.* New Haven: Yale University Press, 1989.

———. *Empires of the Atlantic World.* New Haven: Yale University Press, 2007.

*Espinosa, J. Manuel, trans. and ed. *The Pueblo Indian Revolt of 1696 and the Franciscan Missions in New Mexico.* Norman: University of Oklahoma Press, 1988.

Ferguson, T. J. "Dowa Yalanne: The Architecture of Zuni Resistance and Social Change during the Pueblo Revolt." In *Archaeologies of the Pueblo Revolt: Identity, Meaning, and Renewal in the Pueblo World,* edited by Robert W. Preucel. Albuquerque: University of New Mexico Press, 2002.

Folsom, Franklin. *Indian Uprising on the Rio Grande.* Albuquerque: The University of New Mexico Press, 1973.

*Forbes, Jack D. *Apache, Navaho, and Spaniard.* Norman: University of Oklahoma Press, 1960.

*Gutiérrez, Ramón A. *When Jesus Came, the Corn Mothers Went Away: Marriage, Sexuality, and Power in New Mexico, 1500–1846*. Stanford: Stanford University Press, 1991.

*Hackett, Charles Wilson. *Revolt of the Pueblo Indians of New Mexico and Otermín's Attempted Reconquest, 1680-1682, Volumes 1 and 2*. Albuquerque: University of New Mexico Press, 1942.

Hurtado, Albert L., and Peter Iverson. *Major Problems in American Indian History*. Ann Arbor: University of Michigan Press, 1994.

*James, Harry C. *Pages from Hopi History*. Tucson: The University of Arizona Press, 1974.

John, Elizabeth A. *Storms Brewed in Other Men's Worlds: The Confrontation of Indians, Spanish, and French in the Southwest, 1540–1795*. Norman: University of Oklahoma Press, 1975.

*Kessell, John L. *Kiva, Cross & Crown: The Pecos Indians and New Mexico, 1540–1840*. Tucson: Southwest Parks and Monuments Association, 1987.

Kessell, John L., Rick Hendricks, and Meredith Dodge, eds. *Letters from the New World: Selected Correspondence of Don Diego de Vargas to His Family, 1675–1706*. Albuquerque: University of New Mexico Press, 1992.

*———. *To the Royal Crown Restored: The Journals of Don Diego de Vargas, 1692–1694*. Albuquerque: University of New Mexico Press, 1995.

*———. *Blood on the Boulders: The Journals of Don Diego de Vargas, 1694–1697, Books 1 and 2*. Albuquerque: University of New Mexico Press, 1998.

*Knaut, Andrew L. *The Pueblo Revolt of 1680: Conquest and Resistance in Seventeenth-Century New Mexico*. Norman, OK: University of Oklahoma Press, 1995.

Leeming, David, and Jake Page. *The Mythology of Native North America*. Illustrated by Charles M. Russell. Norman, OK: University of Oklahoma Press, 1998.

Lummis, Charles Fletcher. *The Land of Sunshine*. Cambridge, MA: Harvard University Press, 1899.

Malotki, Ekkehart, ed. *Hopi Tales of Destruction*. Lincoln: University of Nebraska Press, 2002.

Minge, Ward Alan. *Acoma: Pueblo in the Sky*. Albuquerque: University of New Mexico Press, 1991.

*Morrow, Baker H., trans. and ed. *A Harvest of Reluctant Souls: The Memorial of Fray Alonso de Benevides, 1630*. Boulder: University of Colorado Press, 1996.

Noble, David Grant. *Pecos Ruins: Geology, Archaeology, History, and Prehistory*. Santa Fe: Ancient City Press, 1993.

*Ortiz, Alfonso, volume editor. *Southwest, Volume 9, Handbook of North American Indians*. Washington, DC: Smithsonian Institution, 1979.

———. *Southwest, Volume 10, Handbook of North American Indians*, Washington, DC: Smithsonian Institution, 1983.

Page, Jake. *In the Hands of the Great Spirit*. New York: The Free Press, 2003.

Page, Susanne, and Jake Page. *Hopi*, New York: Harry N. Abrams, 1982.

———. *Navajo*, New York: Harry N. Abrams, 1995.

*Preucel, Robert W., ed. *Archaeologies of the Pueblo Revolt: Identity, Meaning, and Renewal in the Pueblo World*. Albuquerque: University of New Mexico Press, 2002.

Ramenofsky, Ann F. *Vectors of Death: The Archaeology of European Contact*. Albuquerque: University of New Mexico Press, 1987.

Riley, Carroll L. *Rio del Norte: People of the Upper Rio Grande from Earliest Times to the Pueblo Revolt.* Salt Lake City: University of Utah Press, 1995.

*———. *The Kachina and the Cross: Indians and Spaniards in the Early Southwest.* Salt Lake City: University of Utah Press, 1999.

Sanchez, Jane C. "Spanish-Indian Relations in the Seventeenth Century: The Causes and Results of the Pueblo Revolt in 1680," Paper presented before the Albuquerque Westerners' Corral, October 21, 1999.

*Sanchez, Joseph P. *The Rio Abajo Frontier, 1540–1692.* Albuquerque: The Albuquerque Museum, 1996.

*Sando, Joe S. *Pueblo Nations: Eight Centuries of Pueblo Indian History.* Santa Fe: Clear Light Publishers, 1992.

*Sando, Joe S., and Herman Agoyo, eds. *Po'pay: Leader of the First American Revolution.* Santa Fe: Clear Light Publishing, 2005.

Schaafsma, Polly. *Warrior, Shield, and Star: Imagery and Ideology of Pueblo Warfare.* Santa Fe: Western Edge Press, 2000.

Schroeder, Susan, ed. *Native Resistance and the Pax Colonial in New Spain.* Lincoln: The University of Nebraska Press, 1998.

Scully, Vincent. *Pueblo: Mountain, Village, Dance.* 2nd ed. Chicago: The University of Chicago Press, 1989.

Secakuku, Alph H. *Following the Sun and Moon: Hopi Kachina Tradition.* Flagstaff: Northland Publishing, 1995.

Silverberg, Robert. *The Pueblo Revolt.* New York: Waybright and Talley, 1970.

Simmons, Marc. *Witchcraft in the Southwest.* Lincoln: University of Nebraska Press, 1974.

———. *New Mexico: An Interpretive History,* Albuquerque: University of New Mexico Press, 1988.

*———. *Coronado's Land: Daily Life in Colonial New Mexico.* Albuquerque: University of New Mexico Press, 1991.

———. *Spanish Pathways: Readings in the History of Hispanic New Mexico.* Albuquerque, University of New Mexico Press, 2001.

*Spicer, Edward H., *Cycles of Conquest.* Tucson: The University of Arizona Press, 1962.

*Steele, Thomas J., Paul Rhetts, and Barbara Awalt, eds. *Seeds of Struggle/Harvest of Faith.* Albuquerque: LPD Press, 1998.

Tuchman, Barbara W. *A Distant Mirror: The Calamitous 14th Century.* New York: Alfred A. Knopf, 1978.

*Weber, David J. *The Spanish Frontier in North America.* New Haven: Yale University Press, 1992.

*———, ed. *What Caused the Pueblo Revolt of 1680?* Boston: Bedford/St. Martins, 1999.

Weddle, Robert S. "Domínguez de Mendoza, Juan." *Handbook of Texas Online,* http://tsha.utexas.edu/handbook/articles/DD/fdo52.html.

White, Tim D. *Prehistoric Cannibalism at Mancos 5MTUMR-2346.* Princeton, NJ: Princeton University Press, 1992.

Whiteley, Peter. *Bacavi.* Flagstaff: Northland Press, 1988.

Witherspoon, Gary. "Language and Reality in Navajo World View." In *Handbook of North American Indians,* Vol. 10: *Southwest,* Alfonso Ortiz, ed., 570–578. Washington, DC: Smithsonian Institution, 1983.

Zubrow, Ezra B. W. "Population, Contact, and Climate in the New Mexico Pueblos," *Anthropological Papers of the University of Arizona, Number 42,* Tucson: The University of Arizona Press, 1974.

# *Acknowledgments*

Looking back over a book one has written and seen turned into the printed version, it is humbling to see how many people it actually took to get the job done. The author is not alone but rather surrounded. (And this is aside from the numerous scholars whose work has contributed anonymously to the overall picture.) Among the many folks I am particularly indebted to are Dr. Rick Hendricks, Dr. Bernard Fontana, Dawn Santiago, and Dr. John Kessell, whose ownership of this realm is widely acknowledged. A host of people are to be found in the offices of Rio Nuevo Publishers, working on one or another effort to rid the book of gremlins and to make it clear and virtuous. Among those are Susan Lowell, Jim Turner, and the impossibly patient Aaron Downey. From afar, Nancy Stone and Larry Loendorf helped perfect the breathtaking cover of this book. Numerous Pueblo people and Hopi commentators will remain (as they prefer) anonymous. My wife Susanne, who introduced me to all of this realm, is the inspiration that burns always in my heart. This book is dedicated humbly and happily to the next generation of Pueblo and Hopi children.

# Index